What people are saying about …

BRIMSTONE

"There are not many Christian authors who are willing to tackle some of the hardest realities of faith and life. Hugh continues to impress with his willingness to address the difficult subject of judgment. For better or worse, all of us wrestle with judging others and being judged. Hugh gives a strong account of how the church should engage with the world and how judgment plays into that picture. Catalyst is grateful for writers like Hugh who help us challenge leaders who love the church!"

Tyler Reagin, executive director of Catalyst

"Jesus gave us His mission of seeking and saving the lost, and He gave us Hugh Halter as a voice calling us back to that mission and helping us learn how to do it effectively. Hugh helps us see why the news about God and eternal life truly is good news. Read this book, and let it inspire you to share His news with everyone!"

Vince Antonucci, pastor of Verve Church and
author of *Renegade* and *God for the Rest of Us*

"Hugh is raw and honest even when it's ugly. But I love his style because *Brimstone* is the kind of book that reminds me that it's God's mercy—not my well-fashioned opinions—that will change hearts and transform lives. Read it and weep; you'll be better for it."

Jo Saxton, chair of 3DMovements and
author of *More than Enchanting*

"Today, Jesus's response to sin and sinners would land Him in hot water with the church He died for. He would be on so many blacklists. If the Christian response to this world, its people, and its struggles have left you cold, disillusioned, rejected, or confused, *Brimstone* is the humble, gentle guide you've been looking for. I seriously wish I could force every single person I know to read this. It would absolutely transform our Christian presence and earn us back a hearing with a world that has stopped listening."

Jen Hatmaker, author of
Interrupted and *For the Love*

"Hugh Halter brings attention and light to a much-needed conversation not only in the church but also in society at large today. This book will challenge and inspire you."

Brad Lomenick, founder of Catalyst

"In a day when social media has made it so easy to judge others, Hugh Halter has given us a gift in writing *Brimstone*. Read it and apply it to all you think, write, post, tweet, or do in your journey to becoming a good neighbor."

David Putman, author of *Detox for the Overly Religious*

"When I pick up a book by my buddy Hugh Halter, I expect to be challenged. I expect to be surprised. I expect to learn. And I expect to laugh out loud. But most of all, I expect to see Jesus—His ways and heart—more clearly. *Brimstone* met my expectations and then blew way past them. Prepare to get to know Jesus better when you read this book."

Lance Ford, author of *Revangelical*

"Hugh is one of the most authentic leaders in the missional movement today. In *Brimstone*, he demonstrates (yet again) why this is the case. When we leave the judgment to Jesus, we are freed to be the loving Good News people He intended us to be in the first place. Bring it on!"

Alan Hirsch, award-winning author on missional Christianity, founder of Forge Mission Training Network, and coleader of Future Travelers

"Unfortunately, we have too often used the words of Scripture to pass judgment on others rather than draw them into the ways of Jesus. In *Brimstone*, Hugh provides a much-needed and better way of being Jesus people to the world around us."

Brad Brisco, coauthor of *Missional Essentials* and *The Missional Quest*

"In *Brimstone*, Hugh is at his raw and gutsy best. This challenging book will cause all of us to think twice before picking up a stone of judgment!"

Deb Hirsch, author of *Redeeming Sex* and coauthor of *Untamed*

"I have never liked Hugh all that much. He cusses more than me. Drinks more than me. And acts like Jesus more than me. So I don't care much for this book. Read it … and see what I mean."

Reggie McNeal, author of *Thank God I'm Not Like All These Others*

"Hugh had me at the first two pages! And by 'had' I mean he nailed my pharisaical tendency toward judgment. Then he dug around where that tendency might have its roots and shared how to get it out of my life. I'm indebted to him for the chance to identify our common problem and find its solution by being more authentically human—less judgment and more love. What better way to encounter a real God than with our real selves? This book will not only challenge your mind—it'll change your heart as well."

Danielle Strickland, major in The Salvation Army, church planter, speaker, writer, and justice advocate

BRIM
STONE

BRIM STONE

THE ART AND ACT OF HOLY NONJUDGMENT

HUGH HALTER

David C Cook

transforming lives together

BRIMSTONE
Published by David C Cook
4050 Lee Vance View
Colorado Springs, CO 80918 U.S.A.

David C Cook Distribution Canada
55 Woodslee Avenue, Paris, Ontario, Canada N3L 3E5

David C Cook U.K., Kingsway Communications
Eastbourne, East Sussex BN23 6NT, England

The graphic circle C logo is a registered trademark of David C Cook.

Unless otherwise noted, all Scripture quotations are taken from the Holy Bible, New
International Version®, NIV®. Copyright © 1973, 2011 by Biblica, Inc.® Used
by permission of Zondervan. All rights reserved worldwide. www.zondervan.com.
Scripture quotations marked ASV are taken from the American Standard Version.
(Public Domain.); AMP are taken from the Amplified® Bible. Copyright © 1954,
1987 by The Lockman Foundation. Used by permission. (www.Lockman.org.);
ESV are taken from The Holy Bible, English Standard Version® (ESV®), copyright
© 2001 by Crossway, a publishing ministry of Good News Publishers. Used by
permission. All rights reserved; KJV are taken from the King James Version of the
Bible. (Public Domain.); MSG are taken from *THE MESSAGE*. Copyright © by
Eugene H. Peterson 1993, 2002. Used by permission of NavPress Publishing Group.

LCCN 2014959545
ISBN 978-1-4347-0653-9
eISBN 978-0-7814-1330-5

The author is represented by and this book is published in association with the
literary agency of WordServe Literary Group, Ltd., www.wordserveliterary.com.

The Team: Alex Field, Jamie Chavez, Amy Konyndyk, Karen Athen
Cover Design: Nick Lee
Cover Photo: Shutterstock

Printed in the United States of America
First Edition 2015

1 2 3 4 5 6 7 8 9 10

042515

CONTENTS

ACKNOWLEDGMENTS

I'd simply like to thank a band of friends whom Cheryl and I have come to love as people deeply committed to the family of Jesus but whom we can always let down with, whom we can trust any of our friends to, and who help us keep a sense of humor along the way of real life. I know we are all responsible in some capacity in leadership, in the church, in our families, and in our community, but it's nice to have friends who follow Jesus without all the religious crud. To our Adullam friends who have partied and served with us over this last decade. To my men's group (Jay Pathak, Dave Runyon, Carl Medearis, and Brad Corrigan) that meets only twice a year because we don't like meetings but with whom I processed this book over illegal putt-putt golf. To the "missional family" I've had the privilege of traveling with over this last stretch (Al and Deb Hirsch, Mike and Carolyn Frost, Lance and Sherri Ford, Brad and Mischele Brisco, and Mike and Sally Breen). And to our Austin group, Brandon and Jen Hatmaker, and special thanks to Tray and Jenny Pruet for sharing the fateful night around our fire pit and coming up with the entire outline and title of *Brimstone* in one sitting while staring into the burning cauldron.

Thanks, mates!
Hugh

In a small town there is only one bakery.

Jesus is the baker.

Two gay men walk in and ask Him to bake a cake for their wedding.

Would Jesus bake the cake?

INTRODUCTION

The deadliest Pharisaism today is not hypocrisy,
but unconscious unreality.

—Oswald Chambers

I posted that question on my blog the day the story broke about the Christian bakery owners who refused to bake a wedding cake for a gay couple. Within an hour I received over 4,500 responses. It took a week or so for me to read through most of them, and to my surprise it appeared that good-hearted churchgoing believers were split down the middle. More interesting was the fact that almost every response contained an air of confidence, and often arrogance, as if it was unfathomable not to take that side of the dilemma.

Now, I'll admit I had my own opinion and felt pretty solid on its correctness from both the missiological (how we approach the world) and theological (how we interpret the truth of Scripture) perspectives. Yet as I read many well-reasoned responses from both sides, I found myself saying, "Wow, I never thought of that," or "That's a really unique angle," or "That's hard to argue against." In the end you'll see what I think about this dilemma, but it's more critical to understand that *how* we arrive at our conclusions is as important as the conclusions themselves.

The impact of this question and the struggle I saw on all sides of the issue profoundly affected me, and my strongest emotion was sadness. I realized that we the church—that is, the witnessing community of the gospel worldwide, the ones privileged with the responsibility to show the world who God is, His glory, truth, love, grace, and mercy—seem to have lost our way. We may all agree that all have sinned and fallen short of God's glory, and we may all proclaim with one voice that Jesus's death on the cross is the only way to take care of sin and open up salvation. But beyond that we have lost our influence, our collective voice proclaiming His glory. People can't see God clearly because we keep creating fog banks of failed legalism, self-focused religion, definitions of holiness that extract us from the real world, and fear of our new neighbors because they are not like us. We are not friends of the world, which makes us very unlike Jesus—the one we purport to follow.

What's worse, we often make these prodigious mistakes with a pure heart, fully believing God is on our side. In most church settings, I've often found we laugh about all the judgments we've made, endured, and now find absurd, almost like a badge of honor: "Oh yeah, I used to think I was going to hell if I had a beer or listened to Amy Grant after she 'crossed over.'"

But the laughter has stopped. Just this week two evangelical megachurch pastors were the first to publicly come out in full support of LGBT issues (all that gay stuff). One of those men is a good friend, and I know personally how this decision is ripping apart the church, his own family, and the faith of many who hang perilously between the dock of grace and the dock of truth. It's not funny anymore. Our kids are leaving the church faster than we can produce them because they don't think the church can help them navigate the real issues they face in the ninth-grade hallways. Our empty nesters are leaving just as fast, and with all our collective resources, good Bible teaching, and fabulous programs, we can barely keep up with Islam on conversion growth, even as bad as their street cred is.

What's the problem? What's holding our collective story hostage so that the onlooking world continues to dismiss us as a bunch of unfeeling, unrealistic, under-a-rock avatars?

The answer is *judgment.* The overuse of poor judgment. The underuse of right judgment. And the misuse of people who get caught in the middle.

Your Author Is a Pharisee

As I sit this evening on my front porch overlooking a beautiful valley, I have decided to jot down how many times I judged people today. Just today. I'm embarrassed to bring this up, but you might as well know what a stinker I am.

7:40 a.m.: Heading to Denver International Airport, I try to turn out of my neighborhood onto a busy highway when some Asian lady, who didn't realize she is supposed to let people merge, jams me. I slam on my brakes and come to a complete stop. I yell at the windshield something about driving like a female, especially an Asian female (two knee-jerk judgments I'm still working on getting over).

7:55 a.m.: I'm now making up time on the freeway, and I pass a police officer radaring people for tickets. I mumble, "Not today, sucka." (The cop, in my judgment, is not a human but a robot controlled by Big Brother, out to make our lives more difficult than they already are.)

8:30 a.m.: I'm in the security line, and of course I go to the United Premier line because I have earned a faster jaunt through the security system that the uncaring FAA has in place (another judgment). Today, however, they are rolling out their new random search system, so guess who gets pulled out of the fast lane and into travel purgatory? The sheer number of four-letter words that crash through my hairless melon is staggering.

9:15 a.m.: I'm sitting on a plane in my highfalutin seat, 2B, with extra legroom that I paid for in money, blood, sweat, and tarmac delays over the last ten years. The flight attendant is fetching me my special drink, but my momentary bliss is abruptly halted by the sight of a huge specimen of southern *homo sapien* who apparently hasn't cared enough about his health for the last twenty years. His seat is next to mine, and it's taking WD-40 and a shoehorn to wedge in his supersized caboose. Then our elbows touch. (Aggghhhhh!)

I could keep going. No kidding. About the mother who can't keep her child quiet, about the male flight attendant who of course is flamboyantly gay, about the people who haven't paid me near enough to come speak for them to make up for the misery I am enduring.

You get the point. Most of us can't make it an hour without making a judgment about another person. I clearly can't! So let's talk about what all this stink is about and where all this darn judgment comes from.

Brimstone

I'm not a rock guy *per se,* but I've taken some interest in brimstone. It turns out that when lit, this yellowish "burning stone," primarily made of sulphur, ignites like wax and turns a deep blue color. The fumes are noxious, and if you're around when brimstone flavors the air, it is almost unbearable.

According to Revelation 21:8, it is into a lake of burning brimstone that all the wicked people will swan dive on the final day of judgment. There are many other scriptures on hell we will discuss, but this one in particular is the one that seems to have created a ubiquitous belief that anyone who doesn't pray a prayer of salvation, get their church on, vote Republican, have sex the way we do, vote to the conservative side, and persecute Rob Bell as they should had better get ready for impending and certain doom. This is also where we get the euphemism of "fire and brimstone" preaching. Just as Jonathan Edwards preached on July 8, 1741, in Enfield, Connecticut, a sermon called "Sinners in the Hands of an Angry God," much of the preaching in the history of America is built upon this fiery lake. Today? Well, we're not quite as aggressive in our preaching of sin and coming judgment, but the molten, nauseating bubbles of judgment are still at a solid rolling boil.

We may be more politically correct today, but whether it be the argument over same-sex marriage, legalized abortion, immigration issues, views on poverty, race relations, or simply how your standard evangelical youth group pressures high schoolers to go share their faith before their friends burn in hell, the stench of this impending fire seems to consume every aspect of our faith today.

I'll let you know right now: *Brimstone* is not about how we can properly judge the world. Nor is this another book trying to pick a nice, neat alternative for those who are caught between Rob Bell, John Piper, Mark Driscoll, and Francis Chan. This book is about judging ourselves, the ones who have become the noxious fumes. You and me and people like us who for years have thought our job was to be off-setting, even upsetting, to people so that they might turn from their wicked ways. Clearly it hasn't worked, and it's time to look again, in depth, at the life of Jesus and the Scriptures as best we can. Then we can peer into our own hearts to see if Jesus would approve of what we disapprove of in others.

In a book called *Flesh,* released in 2013, I tried to take a snapshot of many aspects of Jesus's incarnated humanity and flesh it out for us. In short, the book is about discipleship—being one and helping others to do the same. The easiest definition of being a disciple I could give was to pattern our lives after the human life of Jesus. Then I suggested that Jesus was the least judgmental person the world had ever met and that if 1 John 2:6 is serious, then everyone who claims to be a Christian must walk as Jesus walked. This should make the Christian movement—the church—full of the least judgmental people the world has ever known. Right?

As you can imagine I got blacklisted, put on heresy watches, blogged about as a destroyer of the church, and even lost a few friends, all because I suggested that we model our humanity after the humanity of Jesus. If He took on our flesh to reach us, I was hoping we could agree to take on His flesh to have a little better impact on the world around us.

I went further to surmise that in Galatians when Paul said his physical self had been crucified with Christ and he no longer lived his own life but let Christ live in him, it meant that the way Jesus lived on the street was the way Paul was trying to live. Paul went on to say that he would continue to pastor the Galatians "until Christ is formed in [them]" (4:19). I took that to mean spiritual formation, personal holiness, and the search for godliness is not about just growing in head knowledge, deepening our small-group involvement, beefing up our church attendance, or committing to listen only to Christian music (as the largest national Christian radio station challenged its listeners to do). Rather it means Jesus wants us to conform our humanity to how He lived. And if this is going to happen, then the issue of judgment must be front and center. Because it was front and center for Him, and it was the main issue He fought against.

Jesus lived in a time when everything was seen in black and white. But He lived in true Technicolor. The life of the kingdom, the good news of the gospel, the way of the spirit, and the ministry of reconciliation flew in the face of the "biblical ones." Jesus never gave pat answers, He rarely appealed to the "normal" way of thinking, and He always cut to the heart of the matter. In short, Jesus was trying to teach us how to be human and how to live next door to other humans, most of whom have different sexual orientations, different religions, different parenting styles, different everythings. He tightened the distance between the foreigners, fornicators, freaks, and weasels by creating a new people who would be able to walk in good conscience with their own convictions while not passing judgment on the convictions of others. His goal? That we would be true change agents, as He was. And that our ability to change others would be directly tied to how we loved one another and our neighbors.

Disclaimer (Read This If You Are Looking for a Way Out of Reading This)

The issue of judgment is fraught with … well, judgments. Thus, I'm expecting this book to be a tough read for some. My hope is not to give you my opinion but to force us all into a corner so the only person we can take our cues from is Jesus. I have not figured every side of every line on which you could fall. I'm not completely certain I won't someday change my opinion on the issues I'll bring up in this book. For sure, what I'm writing now is not what I used to believe, so I've got to give myself room to grow and learn. I hope you'll view my effort as honest humility and consider me a good friend with whom you can work through tough dilemmas, instead of a know-it-all who is trying to gain converts who know it all.

If you read the opening dilemma and huffed beneath your breath, "Oh, this is easy—a no-brainer if you're *biblical*," I suggest you feed this book to your dog right now because I think you'll face frustration on every page. You see, I wrote this for people like myself who live in the real world and have friends who have real issues, who have family members with issues, and who haven't fig-ured everything out yet. (Did you catch it? My judgment here is that you don't.) The world is fraught with complicated and perplex-ing stories, and if you see the world only through black-and-white lenses, the colorful life and ways of Jesus will be lost on you. Jesus's main problem—the one that got Him killed—was judgment. My guess is that it was because He challenged everyone's judgments, or lack of true judgment. I hope you'll at least suspend yours for the next hundred pages.

I'll let you know right off the bat that I'm a Bible guy. I'm an evangelical in the sense that I believe God inspired the Scriptures to enlighten us in how we are to live, as well as how we are to draw people to Jesus. I believe in the conversion of the heart and soul. As in my own life, I wholeheartedly believe that spiritual rebirth occurs when a man or woman knows intrinsically and intuitively that they have a sin problem and need Jesus's help to deal with it. I also believe in heaven and hell as literal, eternal places. As such I also believe a person must fear God and that this fear will not only bring us wisdom but also keep us from all sorts of evil. So please don't lump me in the wacko, liberal, universalist, "everything-will-work-out" camp (ah, shucks … another judgment). But believe me, as I have laid down my traditions and theological systems, and more importantly as I have made friends with all sorts of "normal people" who don't believe what I believe, I have come to find that Jesus may not approve of many of my conservative evangelical beliefs or behaviors.

In short, my thinking and approach to people has changed and continues to change … and I'm not afraid of that. In fact I'm glad Jesus didn't just judge me and write me off, leaving me to wallow in my messy, pharisaical, sassy pants. He got through to me, and His crazy teaching and even crazier response to sin and sinners continues to woo me toward a better life, gentler and more patient grace, and greater influence.

I hope this book will be a good intensive study on this key aspect of spiritual formation so that the hope of the world and the hope of God for the world—"Christ in you"—will reawaken a beautiful balance between personal holiness and powerful, peaceful engagement with the strange, sometimes scary, often dirty nooks and crannies of wherever you live. For God's glory!

How to Read This

I've often said that meeting one good Jesus follower is not enough to help people hurtle the twelve-foot wall of poor street cred the Christian movement has right now. So even if you align your judgments to function more like Jesus's, it still may not do much good. The world needs to see a bunch of us change together. Only then will we see some real fruit. So it makes sense to read this with a few other people. Maybe grab your small group or a bunch of disconnected friends, and for sure consider inviting some friends who have tapped out of church or have never been a part of the faith. At the end of each chapter I'll give you some prompts you can discuss together without any prep or pre-thinking. Just grab friends and go! The discussions should be lively and real, and I hope you'll find they may even be healing.

1

THE COMING WRATH: HOW DID WE GET SO MEAN?

Let the Lord of the Black Land come forth!
Let justice be done upon him!
—Aragorn, *The Return of the King*

It was an awesome morning. I was loading the bags in the truck to head to the airport with my whole family. Because of our lifelong bout with my son's epilepsy, we had been granted a Make-A-Wish dream. Instead of choosing something dumb, like going to hear Kelly Clarkson live in concert, my son actually picked a Disney cruise through the Bahamas. Oh yeah, baby! The entire gang was locked and loaded; we were excited about every second of this trip. As we approached the Denver International Airport, the kids started to go berserk and apparently so did the amount of pressure I was applying to the gas. As soon as we rounded the corner for our last left turn into the parking garage, I saw a police officer pointing directly at me, and I had to slam on my brakes so as not to run him over (looking back, maybe that would have been a better play). He yelled at me through the window, "Pull over now!"

We made the flight ... well, most of us did. I was so frazzled and bedazzled by the four-hundred-dollar deficit I had just put our family in that I left three bags of luggage strewn about the airport. So when we got to the ticket counter, Cheryl said, "Honey (actually, I think she said *dipstick*), where are all our bags?" The kids and Cheryl got on the flight, but it took me too long to find the three mystery bags, so I had to fly out a few hours later. What a dork.

That moment lives on in infamy in Halter folklore, but not because it was an isolated event. This crud happens all the time! I figure I've been pulled over at least forty times since we stepped foot on Colorado soil twelve years ago. When it happens, my kids don't even say anything anymore. They just keep their headphones in and stare at their iPhones as if nothing strange is occurring. Fortunately I've been let off the hook quite a bit, but every time I have to face that awkward, nauseating feeling of knowing I have no way out but for the mercy of Bill, Dave, Ken, and other officers I now call friends.

Judgment sucks! Especially when you are under it.

I've been a pastor for twenty-five years, but I've also been the friend of many "sinners" for much longer. After thousands of hours conversing with reasonable, intelligent, unchurched folks, I've come to understand their reasons for not joining our movement. And in almost every case it is because they cannot abide the false, intrusive, rather nasty judgment of those inside Christianity. I used to think people would understand that there will always be a few extreme wackos in every religion and would dismiss them like you would any other extremist.

But I now realize Christian judgmentalism is not an isolated incident. It has hit the mainstream and has touched almost every person who has come within earshot of the church or its people. As I said, I am a recovering judge. As such I often find myself upset with or even making judgments about others who have been in rehab before me, as well as the people who never signed up for Pharisees Anonymous. Honestly, the more I work through my own issues, the more I find that I'm actually upset with God. "Seriously, how the heck did You expect normal knuckleheads to figure out the nuances of the law of love with all these darn scriptures on judgment?"

Have you ever had similar thoughts? My guess is you have—so that's probably a good place to start our journey together.

Welcome to Brimstoneville

Here's the story of judgment in a nutshell. Pre-Jesus, God spent a lot of time setting guidelines and laying down moral rails for humans to run on. He carved the Ten Commandments into stone *with His finger*, but His people kept screwing them up. God reminded them over and over that if they stayed within the lines it would go well and life would be bearable, but also that if they strayed, there would be hell to pay. This is where judgment started. As you know, the people of God didn't do too well measuring up to God's standards. And just as God said, it went badly, over and over. Now, God has nothing if not time and energy, but even the most loving father has a limit.

After a long period of allowing actual judges (some of whom failed as well) and after some kings (who also failed), He sent some prophets to remind people of the options before them. But after all attempts failed, He finally got ticked off enough that He stopped talking to them for three hundred years. God put people in a big, fat time-out and took one Himself.

Yeah, I know it doesn't sound too theological, but that's as clear a summary as I can give you. God's wrath was real. It was brought against His people often, and about the only thing that kept them directed toward truth was punishment and fear. My guess is, from the Old Testament writings, God looks pretty rough to a lot of people. But it's because He had to be. We humans were simply that bad.

Fortunately, like a parent who gets exhausted sending a child back into the bedroom as punishment time and time again, God didn't like this system of constant failure and empty sacrifices, and He made a plan to send Jesus in to put an end to this futile system. Jesus's death on the cross put a literal end to God's wrath—not an end to judgment and justice, just an end to the cycle of warning, failure to heed warning, and then God's anger. Through Jesus, wrath is averted. Prior to Jesus, you got what you deserved. After Jesus, you don't get what you deserve. Prior to Jesus, you had to try to pay for your own sin. After Jesus, He covers it for you. Prior to Jesus, you had to micromanage people, constantly comparing your life against others. After Jesus, there is no longer a basis for comparison. As Romans 5:8–9 says, "But God demonstrates his own love for us in this: While we were still sinners, Christ died for us. Since we have now been justified by his blood, how much more shall we be saved from God's wrath through him!"

I once heard that if you have an abusive father, even if he changes, you can't see him as anything different. I bring this up because I recognize it's hard to hear about God not being angry anymore and believe it. And maybe it's even harder to accept that Jesus made this much difference. For now, I'd just ask that you try to let it sink in, and hopefully over the course of our journey together, Jesus will become the new lens through which you see God in total. As Scripture says in Colossians 1:15, "The Son is the image of the invisible God," and as we go through a lot of scriptures after Jesus that continue to speak of judgment and justice, always remember that no matter what we read or how we interpret what we read, if you want to truly know exactly what God is like, what He thinks of us, and how He handles us as we continue to sin, all you have to do is look at the life of Jesus.

In fact, let's just dive right in and take a look at some of the biggies.

> For we must all appear before the judgment seat of Christ, so that each of us may receive what is due us for the things done while in the body, whether good or bad. (2 Cor. 5:10)

> Just as people are destined to die once, and after that to face judgment. (Heb. 9:27)

> This is how love is made complete among us so that we will have confidence on the day of judgment. (1 John 4:17)

If we deliberately keep on sinning after we have received the knowledge of the truth, no sacrifice for sins is left, but only a fearful expectation of judgment and of raging fire that will consume the enemies of God. Anyone who rejected the law of Moses died without mercy on the testimony of two or three witnesses. How much more severely do you think someone deserves to be punished who has trampled the Son of God underfoot, who has treated as an unholy thing the blood of the covenant that sanctified them, and who has insulted the Spirit of grace? For we know him who said, "It is mine to avenge; I will repay," and again, "The Lord will judge his people." It is a dreadful thing to fall into the hands of the living God. (Heb. 10:26–31)

All this is evidence that God's judgment is right, and as a result you will be counted worthy of the kingdom of God, for which you are suffering. God is just: He will pay back trouble to those who trouble you and give relief to you who are troubled, and to us as well. This will happen when the Lord Jesus is revealed from heaven in blazing fire with his powerful angels. He will punish those who do not know God and do not obey the gospel of our Lord Jesus. They will be punished with everlasting destruction and shut out from the presence of the

Lord and from the glory of his might. (2 Thess. 1:5–9)

Wow, that's a lot of brimstone! It's clear that there *will* be judgment in the end. No matter how you view it or how you interpret it, we will face God, and our lives will be reviewed for what they were. And although these scriptures give the initial appearance that we get exactly what we deserve, we must remember that they all fall under a much larger umbrella of grace. Grace is a hard concept to truly get, but it simply means, it must mean, that we really don't get what we deserve but instead get something better.

According to Ephesians 2:8–9, we are saved by simple grace, without any works—and that means our judgment day is not like the ol' Willy Wonka lever that plummets a person downward through the hatch door. There is no arbitrary breakpoint at which God says, "Sorry, Hugh, you just fell one percentage point under the class curve, so you're in the lake." Grace through faith alone is our entrance. Will our lives still be measured? Yep. Will there be some conversation about shortcomings? Probably. Might there be some honors given out, special assignments, withholdings of jewels and crowns based on a job done well or not done well? Maybe, but don't let these concerns spoil the joy of knowing your life will be reviewed and weighed with the perfect judgment of Jesus.

Judgment 101

Here is a definition you get, by the way, when you google *judgment*: "The ability to make considered decisions or come to sensible conclusions." Hmm, that doesn't sound all that bad, does it? I don't think so. Actually, you'd probably agree that judgment in and of itself is good and that if we were able to exercise good judgment, then the world would run a little more smoothly.

Here's another way to think of judgment: after very careful and discerning thought, the conclusion you reach is a judgment. It should be based in wisdom, truth, and knowledge and delivered for the practical good. This is why Jesus still likes and levels judgments, and it's why I personally am glad judgment exists.

Look, I'm glad we have laws. I'm even glad we have attorneys. I'm glad we have some kind of system of justice and places to put people who can't seem to manage life without constant constraint. I'm glad we have juries and actual judges who try to make "right" judgments. If we didn't have these things, you would not want to bring children into this world.

What I *am* arguing for is removing, or at least decreasing, the amount of lousy judgment that we pour over ourselves and, consequently, everyone else. No, our problem is not judgment itself. It's the lack of right discernment, the absence of perfect knowledge, the void of righteous reasoning that creates the buzz saw of trite, dehumanizing black-and-white lines.

When Jesus died on the cross, He put an end to this kind of condemnation, litigation, separation, and poor judgment. The reason for His incarnation (Jesus coming as a human) was so that judgment could be *averted* rather than leveled. As I've grown older, I've noticed that although I'm glad for the checks and balances that exist to keep some bad people from doing bad things, I actually want less judgment than I used to. Not less justice—just more love, more help, more understanding, more mercy.

I was the keynote speaker at the Canadian national Navigators conference in Whistler several years back. It was a beautiful day, so I took my rental car, a Kia Rio (yeah, baby!) for a drive down to Vancouver just for kicks. The Sea to Sky Highway is famous for gorgeous scenery and more epic twists and turns than a Jason Bourne flick, so I decided to push my Rio a bit. The shocks were a bit splashy, but I was rounding those curves like a champ.

Coming out of one bend in the road, I flew past a Royal Canadian Mountie. In my rearview mirror I saw him powerslide into the median and then burn rubber to catch up with me. One hundred yards later, I had stopped and was rolling down my window. My plan was to play the dumb American, but he didn't even let me start. He just screamed, "What are you thinking? You were only four kilometers an hour under the limit that would have forced me to impound this car and take you in!"

I tried to act like I didn't know what a kilometer thingy meant, but he wasn't buying it. "When was the last time you were pulled over in the States?"

"Uhhh, well, about a month ago," I stammered.

He turned to go back to his car, and spit flew out of his mouth as he said, "That's what I thought. I'll be right back." So there I sat, the keynote speaker of a national ministry conference just four hours away from giving another inspirational talk about Jesus.

He came back and said, "Well, the $@%# computer is slow today, and I ain't sitting around here with you any longer. So you're off the hook like a salmon, but slow down this time!" And with that he walked off. I experienced the flood of adrenaline that comes with incredible relief and thankfulness for having been judged correctly but still let off the hook.

Take a quick inventory of where your heart is: Which do you want more, justice or mercy? My guess is, for yourself, you want mercy. But for others … maybe not. Let's keep reading and see if we can discover which God wants more.

Where Bad Judgment Began

Can you imagine a world with absolutely no judgment? Most likely not, because the lack of judgment would also mean that there would be no fear, no insecurity, no offensive behavior, and therefore no need for defensiveness. There would be no need to justify behavior, no need to move aggressively or violently against another person or country. A world without judgment would be as close to perfect as you could dream of.

Well, that's what life without sin would be like. Adam and Eve lived in a perfect paradise like this, fearlessly hanging out with almighty God, walking around naked but without shame. We're not given all the details, but their story gives us some profound ideas of what living in a world without judgment might be like.

Yesterday on a flight to LA, I read an article about nude yoga classes springing up all over the country. As someone who needs to do yoga a couple of times a week to keep my back from locking up, I was utterly amazed that people would actually attempt some of these poses and exercises without cover! Heck, I get insecure just looking at my gnarly toes or back fat in the mirror, so it seems untenable that people could down doggy without a linen saddle on their haunches. I'll admit that to be naked is the most comfortable way to walk around, albeit in one's private residence. But very few people would find it comfortable to walk to the corner strip mall or even to the mailbox without clothing. Likewise, it is almost impossible to picture Adam and Eve without any sense of embarrassment or shame. But they were, at least before sin.

But sin happened. Adam and Eve listened to themselves and to Satan, and immediately after eating the fruit, they became aware of their nakedness. They hid from God, and for the first time in the history of the universe there was blame, justification of behavior, comparison, and denial of truth. Judgment, both from God and from humanity, entered the scene.

How did sin—the root of judgment—win the day? Because Satan challenged the issue of the knowledge of good and evil: "Did God really say …?" He knew that the knowledge of good and evil is the basis for judgment. God, of course, had this knowledge and, without needing to disclose all the details, was able to warn Adam and Eve that it would be very bad for them. Maybe if He had explained it better they would have thought more carefully about what would happen if they ate the fruit. Even so, Satan's lie, coupled with the natural human hunger for knowledge, still would have been too strong. Since then, sin has twisted what it means to know the difference between good and evil. We like the idea that we can know more than the next guy, that we can use it to get a leg up, to dominate and win. But mostly we don't want to have to rely on or trust in God to make the final call—we'd rather be the final authority.

So where does the story go from here? Downhill fast. As humans tried to judge each other, they got it wrong time and time again. The result was murder, strife, war, and all the evil that comes from these things. Oh, they knew more than they did before the fall, and they were even able to expose more wrongdoing than before, but their sinful nature tainted their ability to judge good and evil. They couldn't even judge themselves, much less anyone else, aright.

The only reason humans didn't completely annihilate themselves was the religious system of the Law we've already discussed. But this system of commandments required people to administer judgment and handle all the means of sacrificing to appease God's anger. And that was a colossal debacle. God's ten laws were turned into thousands of laws, and His simple judgments got replaced by confusing human judgments that grew harsher and harsher. People were not only bad at keeping commandments; they were even worse at helping others keep them.

You Don't Want to Know

One time I was pressing my wife for info about the guys my two girls were dating. I think I was just having a normal dad breakdown moment, and I was concerned about how into these guys my girls were, whether or not I needed to put a hit out on the youngsters— you know, standard dad stuff. My wife kept encouraging me to back off and just let her handle it, but I kept badgering her. She finally said, "Okay, if I tell you a little, I'm going to tell you everything. But you'd better be ready for everything."

"Of course I'm ready," I said.

She gave me that look—you know the one—and asked, "Are you? Do you really want to know every little detail of their emotions and actions?"

For some reason the way she asked this made me do something out of character—I actually listened and thought about it! Then I said, sheepishly, "Actually, don't tell me. I don't wanna know anything. You handle it."

Well, this is really the story behind God's forbidden fruit. I've always wondered what God was afraid of, and when I hear Satan's lie, I actually sort of agree with him: Why *doesn't* God want us to know everything? Why doesn't He let us know the differences between good and evil? Now I get it. God knew it was simply too much info for us to handle, and history has proven it a few kabillion times over. The most dangerous knowledge in the world is the knowledge of good and evil for one glaring reason: we don't steward the knowledge well at all. Most of the time we get it wrong, and when we do, we really make things worse.

May I talk about myself for just a minute? I think, generally speaking, I'm a pretty good guy. I sincerely walk with the Lord, I'm honest about my shortcomings, and I have no problem asking for forgiveness. I almost always want the best for people, and I try not to go more than fifteen miles per hour over the speed limit. I'm also aware of the Enemy's tactics, I usually pray about my decisions, and I ask for God's blessing and wisdom. But looking back over all my judgments about people and situations (like that morning in the Introduction), I've come to realize that I bat about .500. In the world of baseball, I'd be a leadoff hitter and make the Hall of

Fame, but in the world of people, that means I misjudge everyone and everything half the time. That means I screw up half the people I try to help!

Again, all this gives us a pretty good idea of why Jesus came to earth. He came to relieve us from having to make the call on ourselves and others. He came to remove the connection between sin and judgment. In fact, He came to take judgment back. The doctrine of the incarnation of Jesus is that He came to earth to die for sin, yes, but beyond the cross His intention was to model a new form of humanity that, according to John 1:14, would again, as it was before sin, be full of grace and full of truth all at the same time. Sure, the incarnation is about atonement, but remember that atonement was never the end goal. Atonement, that is the payment for sin, was ultimately for the purpose of redemption and reconciliation. As 2 Corinthians 5:19 says, "God was reconciling the world to himself in Christ, not counting people's sins against them. And he has committed to us the message of reconciliation."

Through Jesus, judgment has been redeemed, bought back, and administered correctly through eyes of love rather than eyes of fear. Yes, the scripture verses I began this chapter with, when put together, seem to let us know that God is a just God and that we should fear Him and fear deeply our own way of sin. But as we put these scriptures together with the game-changing reality of Christ's death on the cross for failing sinners, we must let Jesus's payment for sin trump our failures in sin. That's the gospel. I fit every warning in those scriptures. I do trample underfoot the grace of Jesus. I do keep sinning, and sometimes I even know I'm about to do this and still choose to. I don't always align my life to the gospel. And, yes, I think it's okay to look up and fear God. But as I look up in fear, the story of Jesus seems to scream and plead that Jesus averts the lightning bolts. Jesus could have come to condemn, and I surely would have been one worthy of it. Yet He didn't come to condemn but to save. Whew.

So does a judgment day happen for us? Yes, but now we may see that time as simply the day we all meet Jesus and thank Him for averting the judgment we had coming. All of us.

Let's look at how this plays out in the next chapter.

What do we know for sure?

- Judgment is real. God doesn't like sin or how it affects our ability to judge between good and evil.
- Not all judgment is bad. Good judgment, which is what God uses, is always good for people.
- People aren't good; we're sinful, and sin makes most of our judgments wrong. The world is torn apart through dissention, wars, and even church issues because of wrong judgments.
- God wants to relieve people of having to be the final judge.
- Religious judgment is the hardest to get right and thus the easiest place to miss the gospel of Jesus.

What should we change in light of what we know?

- What is your batting average: How often have you been wrong in judging people? Can you share one example?

Who might this change affect, and what is God asking you to do?

- What has been the result of your judgment? Did anyone get hurt? Do you have any unresolved relationship conflicts because of bad calls?
- Consider writing some e-mails or setting a coffee time simply to say you're sorry. See what happens in this simple act of nonjudgment.

Why is this good news for you?

- You don't need to live under the pressure of having to fix the world's problems, or even the problems of the neighbor next door.
- As a parent or close friend, this allows you to influence people, even your own children, with humility and teachability.
- You may begin to see estranged or strained relationships begin to heal.

- Instead of erring toward harsh judgment, you can remember how much of your own sin Jesus covers and extend the same leash to others that He gives to you.

2

THE COMING SON: WHO GETS THE GAVEL?

There are just some kind of men who—who're so busy worrying about the next world they've never learned to live in this one, and you can look down the street and see the results.
—Harper Lee, *To Kill a Mockingbird*

This week marks the twelfth week since the Ferguson race riots started. Since then, police have been shot while sitting in their squad cars, protests continue, fires still burn, and there seems to be no end in sight. Extremists on both sides seem to always fan the flames of divide, but even in the middle, with reasonable adults, judgments seem to be insurmountable. Police in New York City are now leveling complaints against their own leaders, and around dinner tables like my own, I find that opinions people have are hard to change.

Here's a scientifically and sociologically proven fact about adults: our biases are almost impossible to change once they're set. A trial lawyer I know says that people see what they already believe, and the job of a great attorney is to convince people to see beyond their existing beliefs.

Apparently, there are only two ways to change a bias: One is by having an experience that is so emotional it changes your perspective. The other is by listening to someone you trust to be an authority. We all respect certain people to the extent that their opinion sways our own. For instance, in the world of theology and doctrine, I've come to trust men like Tim Keller and N. T. Wright. When I want some marriage advice, I go to a guy named Greg. I go with Bobby Flay when it comes to cooking, my local weatherman with weather, and with political decisions I go with Stephen Colbert. He cracks me up, but also for some reason I always pick his side. When I'm not sure, I go with what these people say. Not sure why, I just do.

When it comes to making sound judgments about the choices people make, out there in the world and especially in your life, you've got to decide whose opinion you're going to be influenced by. Who will you really trust to make the right call? Your pastor? A popular blogger? Maybe even the apostles Paul or Peter? Those may all be good options, but I suggest letting Jesus be the one with the gavel.

Listen to this:

> Moreover, the Father judges no one, but has entrusted all judgment to the Son, that all may honor the Son just as they honor the Father.

Whoever does not honor the Son does not honor the Father, who sent him. Very truly I tell you, whoever hears my word and believes him who sent me has eternal life and will not be judged but has crossed over from death to life. Very truly I tell you, a time is coming and has now come when the dead will hear the voice of the Son of God and those who hear will live. For as the Father has life in himself, so he has granted the Son also to have life in himself. And he has given him authority to judge because he is the Son of Man. Do not be amazed at this, for a time is coming when all who are in their graves will hear his voice and come out—those who have done what is good will rise to live, and those who have done what is evil will rise to be condemned. By myself I can do nothing; I judge only as I hear, and my judgment is just, for I seek not to please myself but him who sent me. (John 5:22–30)

Doesn't it sound like two CEOs of a company minimizing their own authority and graciously giving preference to the other? Apparently both Jesus and the Father have the rightful claim to life and wisdom and judgment. Both are equally God. Both are equally perfect. Both of them have full knowledge of every heart and every situation. Neither of them has selfish or impure motives, and they each desire to bring glory and honor to the other. They stand together in love and judgment.

But the important thing is the Father has given Jesus the authority, the power, to judge. I'm not sure how the conversation went down, but maybe the Father said, "Son, You're the one who has to take on the flesh of humanity, submit to the curse of work, pour Your life out for the whole world, carry the sin and death of every human on Your back, and then die for them ... so You get to make the call."

Isn't that comforting? It's such good news for a cat like me. The only one who busted a way out of Brimstoneville is also the only one who gets to judge me in the end. Not my brothers and sisters who've labeled me a heretic, not my colleagues or friends who love me, not my kids or even my wife. And here's the real kicker—in the end, for better or worse, I don't get to judge myself either.

But it goes the other way too. I have developed prejudices throughout my life about people who look or act differently from what I think is "right." I have theological, political, and social biases based on what I've studied, learned, and experienced. And, as you saw at the beginning of the book, I pass judgment on people left and right. Do I have the authority or power to do this? Clearly, no. If I won't let anyone judge me other than Jesus, maybe it's time to consider that my judgments about others should be left under His gavel as well.

Who will you trust to help you change your natural biases toward people? Who will you defer to when you're frustrated and want to end a relationship? Who will you ask for wisdom when your gay cousin invites you to attend his wedding? When you hear stories about race-fueled violence in Ferguson, Missouri, who will you turn to for guidance about an appropriate reaction? The answer, of course, is Jesus, but don't write it off in the obvious Sunday school way, when the answer to every question is "Jesus." This is life-changing—no, *world*-changing—stuff.

So Jesus is the only one who gets to pass judgment. He gets the gavel. Philippians 2:10–11 declares, "At the name of Jesus every knee should bow, in heaven and on earth and under the earth, and every tongue acknowledge that Jesus Christ is Lord, to the glory of God the Father."

In other words, once you've given your life to Jesus, He gets to rule over your life. Not Fox News, not CNBC, not CNN, not your pastor, priest, or parents. Jesus is more authoritative than anyone. His goals and interests in the world must become more important than your own, His character should start to show up in your character, and how He treats people must be the plumb line by which you now relate to others. Especially those pesky "sinners."

So let's take a look at how Jesus judges people. John 8:12–18 says,

> When Jesus spoke again to the people, he said, "I am the light of the world. Whoever follows me will never walk in darkness, but will have the light of life." The Pharisees challenged him, "Here you are, appearing as your own witness; your testimony is not valid." Jesus answered, "Even if I testify on my own behalf, my testimony is valid, for I know where I came from and where I am going. But you have no idea where I come from or where I am going. You judge by human standards; I pass judgment on no one. But if I do judge, my decisions are true,

because I am not alone. I stand with the Father, who sent me. In your own Law it is written that the testimony of two witnesses is true. I am one who testifies for myself; my other witness is the Father, who sent me."

Whoa, hold up a second. Jesus has the authority to judge, and He judges correctly, but He generally chooses not to judge people? He can make right judgments if He wants to, but His intent is not to use His authority to "get us." There's no condemnation in His judgment! Did you catch that? He doesn't come into the world with the desire to punish us or push us into the lake of burning brimstone. His intention is exactly the opposite—He came to save. This is a really important nuance about Jesus that we often miss. Most of us feel it is our job to rid the world of evil, to call it out, to rant and rave over all the bad stuff people do. But Jesus didn't come with this posture toward people or political aggravations.

John 3:16–18 gives us a little more insight:

> For God so loved the world that he gave his one and only Son, that whoever believes in him shall not perish but have eternal life. For God did not send his Son into the world to condemn the world, but to save the world through him. Whoever believes in him is not condemned, but whoever does not believe stands condemned already because they have not believed in the name of God's one and only Son.

Again we see that judgment and even condemnation exist, but only because of how we judge ourselves. Jesus doesn't judge, because He doesn't need to. It's like coming upon a drunk, stinky bum in the streets who's missing most of his teeth. I don't need to tap him on the shoulder and proclaim to him that he is a substance abuser who has screwed up his life. All he has to do is walk by a big store window. Then he will stand condemned by what he sees in the reflection.

John 3:19 says it this way (and notice all four translations):

And this is the condemnation, that light is come into the world, and men loved darkness rather than light, because their deeds were evil. (KJV)

And this is the judgment, that the light is come into the world, and men loved the darkness rather than the light; for their works were evil. (ASV)

The [basis of the] judgment (indictment, the test by which men are judged, the ground for the sentence) lies in this: the Light has come into the world, and people have loved the darkness rather than and more than the Light, for their works (deeds) were evil. (AMP)

This is the crisis we're in: God-light streamed into the world, but men and women everywhere ran for the darkness. They went for the darkness because they were not really interested in pleasing God. Everyone who makes a practice of doing evil, addicted to denial and illusion, hates God-light and won't come near it, fearing a painful exposure. But anyone working and living in truth and reality welcomes God-light so the work can be seen for the God-work it is. (vv. 19–21, MSG)

This is a very unique point about how we are to relate to people who are screwing up their lives or the lives of others. We may have enough knowledge to make a correct judgment over them, but if we take our cues from Jesus, we will realize we don't need to impose our judgment. Eventually every sin will be uncovered, and in time people will confront their sin all on their own. If we judge them, our condemnation might make them flee back into the dark, but if we stand in God's light without condemnation, He may use us to encourage others to come out of the dark. I'll admit, I struggle with this. I have always believed that Christians are to stand against evil. We are supposed to go after the bad guys. We are called by God to stand up for truth as we know it, even if in doing so we have to take up arms. Yet if Jesus is my Lord, I must heed His words in Matthew 5:38–45:

You have heard that it was said, "Eye for eye, and tooth for tooth." But I tell you, do not resist an evil person. If anyone slaps you on the right cheek, turn to them the other cheek also. And if anyone wants to sue you and take your shirt, hand over your coat as well. If anyone forces you to go one mile, go with them two miles. Give to the one who asks you, and do not turn away from the one who wants to borrow from you.

You have heard that it was said, "Love your neighbor and hate your enemy." But I tell you, love your enemies and pray for those who persecute you, that you may be children of your Father in heaven.

Most take this passage in the context of physical confrontations, but I believe Jesus was giving us a new way of influencing those who see the world from a position of darkness. You see, people are not evil. Evil is a spiritual force that often controls people or blinds people or causes people to do evil things. But darkness is never driven out by darkness. People have the lightbulbs turned on only when they see the light in us. And light doesn't have to confront to do its work. It just has to be there.

We will dive a little deeper into this later, but for now it's pretty clear we should not be the one with the gavel, the rock, or the red and blue lights on the top of our car. Jesus is the only one who gets to judge, but He doesn't—so neither should we.

When Jesus Does Judge

So you might be thinking, *Okay, so Jesus can judge us but doesn't, so does that mean no one ever gets judged? And is that actually good? Doesn't there have to be human judgment so things don't go berserk?* We've already shown that judgment, if done well, is a corrective measure and that the knowledge of good and evil, in the right hands, is good.

In John 9, we have a powerful story of Jesus meeting a man who was blind from birth. Jesus's own disciples asked what seems like a really horrible question, even though to them it naturally rose from their Jewish biases:

"Rabbi, who sinned, this man or his parents, that he was born blind?"

"Neither this man nor his parents sinned," said Jesus, "but this happened so that the works of God might be displayed in him" (vv. 2–3).

Jesus then spit on the ground to make some mud, smeared the man's eyes with it, told him to go wash in a local pool, and *whamo!*, he could see. When the man went home, his friends and neighbors all marveled and wondered if it was the same man they had seen begging all of his life. They couldn't figure it out, so they made the mistake of bringing him before the Pharisees, who, of course, questioned and berated the man because Jesus had healed him on the Sabbath. They said, "This man is not from God, for he does not keep the Sabbath" (v. 16).

After all this, the man saw Jesus again and put his faith in Him. Then Jesus made this interesting statement: "For judgment I have come into this world, so that the blind will see and those who see will become blind" (v. 39).

Did Jesus change His tune? He said before that He didn't come to judge, but now He says that He did come into the world to judge. What's the deal?

It is simply this: He did not come to condemn people who are stuck and struggling with sin. But in regard to all the misuse and abuse of people and to Satan's work to thwart God's plans, Jesus did come to bring light and judgment. In other words, He didn't come into the world to judge, but He did come so that judgment would occur.

Consider John 12:31: "Now is the time for judgment on this world; now the prince of this world will be driven out."

Interesting—judgment is aimed at Satan, not us!

Several years ago, I was invited to share the story of God in an old pub in Denver. The owners were not Christians, but they liked me well enough to not only serve beers during my six-hour presentation but also to interact with it. A few months later, I asked one of the gals what she had felt about all the Jesus talk. She said, "Actually, I loved it, and you totally had me for the first three hours. But then you lost me."

Bummed out and curious, I said, "When? What did I say?"

"Well, it was in that part where you were talking about Jesus coming to die for our sins so that evil could be judged in the world." I was perplexed, so I just raised my eyebrows a bit to ask her to tell me more. "Yeah, I mean, I get that there is evil, but I just can't picture God doing anything but pure love. I just don't think He would even judge Satan."

As we talked more about all the incredible atrocities done in the world—from sex trafficking, to war crimes, to physical and sexual abuse in families and churches, to school shootings—I asked, "Don't you want to see this fixed, or at least see the tide of abuse stemmed in the world?" She finally agreed that she did want justice to happen. And in this we now see why Jesus still brings judgment—He will judge Satan and the works of evil in the world. The gavel does come down, but before you take joy in this, remember that sometimes even we who love God work with the Enemy.

In John 16:7–11, we read,

> But very truly I tell you, it is for your good that I am going away. Unless I go away, the Advocate will not come to you; but if I go, I will send him to you. When he comes, he will prove the world to be in the wrong about sin and righteousness and judgment: about sin, because people do not believe in me; about righteousness, because I am going to the Father, where you can see me no longer; and about judgment, because the prince of this world now stands condemned.

Again, we see that judgment is meant to condemn Satan and his minions, but we also see that Jesus came into the world to straighten out people who are wrong about sin and righteousness and judgment. And I don't know any other group of people who have been more culpable for wielding a wrong sword than us in the church. That means Jesus came to straighten us out too, and it's not far-fetched to say that Christian judgment is a key tool the Enemy has been using to keep people in the dark for generations.

What do we know for sure?

- Jesus is the only final, and safe, authority and judge.

- Judgment is good if it leads to justice and redemption. It is for this reason that Jesus came into the world.
- Judgment without these intents or ends is not good and is actually counterproductive to God's kingdom design.
- People are already under judgment even without you judging them. They are either hiding in the dark or walking toward the light.
- Jesus really came to judge Satan and bad judges (which includes many Christians).

What should we change in light of what we know?

- Consider the biases you grew up with about "sinners." Take a moment to make a list of the judgments you now look back on as wrong, or at least insensitive.

Who might this change affect, and what is God asking you to do?

- Who have you imposed your judgments on?
- What has been the result?
- Do you see justice or redemption, or a lack of relationship?

Why is this good news for you?

- You no longer have to worry about pointing out people's darkness.
- You get to live as light and draw people to the light, where Jesus can naturally change them.

3

DON'T BE A STONER: TIME TO DROP THE ROCKS

We should be rigorous in judging ourselves
and gracious in judging others.
—John Wesley

A famous—and to some, infamous—pastor is kicked out of the church-planting organization he started and is also asked to step down from his post in his own church. Your "progressive Christian" friend starts a hot conversation about this pastor *on your Facebook timeline*; some participants are crowing triumphantly over his fall, while others are shocked that a man who preached the gospel so well would be treated so harshly.

Another conservative church just announced it has changed its stance on LGTB issues and will now be ordaining gay clergy and performing same-sex marriages.

You're at your neighbor's house having dinner when your hosts mention that the new neighbors across the street are a "lesbo" couple with two young adopted children. They make a few other comments about the neighborhood going to hell in a hand basket as they pour you another drink.

A Muslim family with kids the same age as your own moves into the neighborhood. As they unload the moving truck, your kids connect, and then Hassim asks if your little Johnny can come over for a playdate.

You hear from your daughter, who is in college, that her friend needs a place to live. The friend is a nineteen-year-old with a "messed-up life" and a four-year-old daughter, both essentially her fault, of course, but your daughter now wants you to help out.

Robin Williams just committed suicide. Folks in your church are writing blogs about how those who commit suicide make the most selfish choice and always go to hell. They ask you to post comments about your opinion.

Do you associate with them or not? Do you let your children associate with them or not? Do you bail them out of their jams or not? Do you make snide comments, or do you stick up for them? Do you take up the long-term project of befriending them and helping them get healthy, or do you justify your lack of concern and action because if they got themselves *into* their messes, they need to get themselves *out*? In other words, do you make judgments and stand apart from them, or do you advocate for them?

We've all found ourselves in situations like these, to some extent. The common denominator in all these scenarios is that *you have to choose a side*. You can't stay neutral. Or at least that's what you feel.

So far, we've settled some issues. First, there is judgment and there needs to be. Second, Jesus is the only one who judges correctly all the time, and thus we need to let His biases win out over our own biases. As we move on, it's important we take at least a moment to scroll through our memory banks and acknowledge how many of our own judgments we may have to put in the Never Use Again file. Here are a few fun ones from my past:

- Making fun of Amy Grant and Michael W. Smith because they "crossed over" and did a few secular songs. Then justifying my correct judgment by smirking when Amy divorced and remarried. "Yeah, see, I knew she was walking away from God."
- Writing people off and assuming they were leaving the faith because they got divorced.
- Concluding that other Christians were "barely in" because they listened to secular music.
- Fighting with other Christian friends over whether or not Bono and Mumford & Sons were Christians because they dropped the F-bomb.
- Lamenting Christian television and radio programs for watering down the gospel, wasting people's money, or flat-out being weird.

- Believing it is impossible to be a Christian and vote Democrat.

- Believing it is impossible to be a Christian and vote Republican (still squishy on that).

- Believing no one who commits suicide goes to heaven.

- Believing, spiritually speaking, that everyone is off scot-free until the age of accountability. (Who the heck made that up? Interestingly, the age of accountability for many denominations is fifteen, for the Nazarenes it's twelve, and for Southern Baptists it's seven. Dang, those SBs are tough!)

- Thinking that only a small percentage of Christians are actually Christians. (Since the course I took on New Testament theology had a two-week focus on Christian carnality right after the three-week intensive on the doctrine of election, I was coerced into believing this.) I also thought that a good chunk of the ones who made it got to be complete buttheads and could sin their faces off without any retribution.

- Deciding, based on no scientific or sociological evidence whatsoever, that all gay people choose to be gay and that no one is born gay.

- Believing most Muslims agree with *jihad* (which, in America, is defined as terrorism), whether they participate or not.

- Before I was a pastor, thinking all pastors were self-seeking glory hounds.
- Now that I'm a pastor, thinking all parishioners are slack, halfhearted consumers.

I'm not sure if my list helped jar some of your own judgments loose, but it's clear we all have a long list. It's just natural to pick up rocks and want to throw them, isn't it?

Do You Stay or Do You Go?

In John 8:1–11, we have a profound illustration of judgment. A woman, most likely in her late twenties, is dragged out of an alleyway and into the middle of the synagogue where Jesus has been teaching. Men are pointing and yelling, "Whore … slut … sinner!" A crowd is drawn into the synagogue so they can participate in the melee.

Imagine you are there. You try to avoid the scene, but without warning someone grabs you and hands you a rock the size of a loaf of bread. You try to walk the other way, but now the crowd is mushrooming, and a tide of humanity forces you to the front row, just a few feet from the woman. Without wanting to be there, you are in the eye of the storm—the storm of religious philosophy, long-held laws of Moses, and spiritual leaders you've tried faithfully to emulate.

Now you look at this woman. You can't quite see her face because she's kneeling in the dust, sobbing, covering her head as she waits for boulders to crush her skull. How are you supposed to feel right now, especially since you've tried to live above the standards to which she's apparently lowered herself? Your first instinct is to get out of there. It's just too harsh, way over the top, but ... her sin is really bad and the crowd seems set on making her an example to others. Maybe you think, *Well, she knew better and still chose to fornicate,* so for the moment you hold on to the stone that is now clammy and cold in your hand.

Strangely the crowd settles down as Jesus finally moves from where He was teaching. He doesn't seem bothered by the pressure and the screams; in fact, He walks as if He can't even hear the crowd or the religious leaders yelling at Him. His eyes are fixed on the heap of woman hunched over in the dirt. He gently puts His right hand on her heaving back and kneels down next to her. As He comforts her, He seems to write something in the dirt. You can't make it out, but He stops and stands when the priests force Him to make a statement about her sin. Everyone who had been drawn to His teaching is breathless, waiting to hear what He will say about the Law of Moses and its clear teaching about this woman's sin and punishment.

With what appears to be a confident smirk on His face, He quiets the crowd with words you never expected: "All right, but let the one who has never sinned throw the first stone!" Then He stoops down again to write in the dust. When the accusers hear this, they slip away one by one, beginning with the oldest, until only Jesus is left standing with the woman. "Where are your accusers?" Jesus asks. "Didn't even one of them condemn you?"

"No, Lord," she says.

And Jesus says, "Neither do I. Go and sin no more."

As an onlooker, someone right in the middle of this, my guess is you would have known you'd sinned, so you'd have dropped the rock. But if I were there, I'd also wonder, *Is that the right thing to do? Isn't her sin worse than mine? Shouldn't she pay a price for the pain she's caused?*

I'd also think, *We shouldn't be this brutal, but this isn't a debatable matter. She was caught in some real sin, and other people will take it lightly if we don't judge and condemn her. That's what the Law of Moses, handed down by God, tells us to do. If we don't take a stand on this sin, we're surely going to slide down a slippery slope of social debauchery.*

Maybe due to peer pressure and not wanting to be the only one *not* to leave, I suppose I'd file out like the rest of them. But I think there would have been many circles of people outside the synagogue babbling to themselves, trying to make sense of what they had just experienced.

What Jesus did went against all of their ingrained religious biases.

Pick a Card

Before you hastily drop your rocks, I want to make sure you really feel good about it. Most people live with a deep sense of insecurity, self-loathing, and unworthiness. When we bring these broken identities to Jesus, He heals us; if we don't, then we mask our pain behind judgments over others. This is why people are drawn to gossip or the latest tabloid dirt on a small scale and become racist bigots on a large scale. We just love to see people who are worse than we are so that in our surface comparisons we come out smelling just a little less musty. We pick up rocks because they feel good in our hands.

For fun, take a look at the following two people. Obviously God has no favorites, but try to pick the one person you think Jesus would choose as an example for Christians to follow.

Susan the Agnostic

Susan's dad used to be a pastor of a small church in Mobile, Alabama. Around age eighteen, Susan began to attend church less and less, though, because she grew tired of the consistent hypocrisy and unloving attitude so many in the church had. She brought some of her friends to church, but racist taunts and social cliques made her vow to never do it again. As she grew older, she never lost faith that Jesus died for her sins, but she just couldn't see that He changed people. She left home and the church and joined the Peace Corps. After working in some of the world's most impoverished places, Susan committed her life to sharing in their poverty until she retired at the age of fifty-two. Over those years, Susan remained single, had many relational and sexual experiences, and shared an occasional joint of marijuana, but she was generally beloved by everyone who met her. After she retired, Susan came back to the States, lived in a double-wide mobile home, worked at Starbucks for nine dollars an hour, and continued to volunteer among the poor until she died at age sixty-one from AIDS, which she contracted while working in an Algerian hospital back in her thirties.

Billy the Bible Guy

Billy grew up in a solid Christian home. His parents passed down a robust knowledge of the Bible and Christian morality, so Billy was a consistent churchgoer, loved to worship through song, tithed faith-fully, had an hour-long devotion every morning, and never slept with girls as he grew up. He taught Sunday school and small groups and became an elder in his church. Billy became a successful businessman who funded many church-planting efforts and gifted many kids with scholarships to church camp. He was well respected by everyone in the church community. Interestingly, Billy spent almost his entire life without any friends outside the church, and he didn't even know much about his own neighbors. He wouldn't call himself racist, but he did believe that poor people didn't work hard enough, and he felt a bit uncomfortable around people of any color different from his own.

ᶔᴥᴥ

You know I'm stacking the deck here, but maybe you're catching a key point. Jesus views people in really strange ways. Growing up, I would have picked Billy as closest to the ideal, but I'd have asked him to work on his view of outsiders. I would have considered sleep-ing around or smoking pot signs that someone was quite far from God. Yet as we look at what Jesus emphasizes as true marks of love, traits He wants to see in us, you can't help but reconsider Susan as someone Jesus really loves, and even likes.

Matthew 9:10–11 says, "While Jesus was having dinner at Matthew's house, many tax collectors and sinners came and ate with him and his disciples. When the Pharisees saw this, they asked his dis-ciples, 'Why does your teacher eat with tax collectors and sinners?'"

This would have been a normal question for those who focused their lives on outward holiness. How could Jesus, a holy man, hang out with these people whose sin was so obvious and causing so many social problems? In consistent fashion, Jesus kicked them below the belt by saying, "It is not the healthy who need a doctor, but the sick. But go and learn what this means: *'I desire mercy, not sacrifice.'* For I have not come to call the righteous, but sinners" (vv. 12–13, emphasis mine).

What does this statement mean—mercy, not sacrifice?

Sacrifices are those things we do as religious responses to God. In the Old Testament, sacrifices occurred most often in the context of temple worship to appease the judgment of God. People would burn animal sacrifices, bring firstfruit offerings, and perform cleansing rituals. All of these were in an attempt to be approved by God and cleared by other people. Sacrifices may have had healthy elements to them, but, as so often happens with people, they were twisted into the means by which people were judged to be in or out, good or bad, acceptable or condemnable. This is probably why Jesus went berserk in the temple, whipping up a frenzy and overturning tables. He hates it when people replace a heart-level faith with religious protocol.

And the heart is exactly what is at the center of mercy. Mercy assumes mistakes have been made. Mercy expects people to screw up, and rather than grinding them into the dirt for it, mercy grants them what they need to heal. With mercy, there is no clean or unclean— instead there are just people who need a break.

Sadly, we have to admit that our definition of a "good Christian" is most often lodged in the camp of sacrifice rather than the camp of mercy. Billy nails it at sacrifice but sucks rocks at mercy. And when you suck rocks at mercy, you tend to become someone who likes to chuck rocks at others.

Jesus has to suggest we learn what *mercy* means because it's not our natural perspective. Christians still focus on religious sacrifices, but we won't get it right until we see the world through the eyes of mercy.

Maybe Jesus wants sacrifices of mercy to be what it means to follow Him. Now that troublesome scripture in James 1:27 makes some sense: "Religion that God our Father accepts as pure and faultless is this: to look after orphans and widows in their distress and to keep oneself from being polluted by the world." Again, we see mercy's connection to sacrifice. In other words, instead of bringing your tithes and offerings and lifting your hands during worship, consider, or *learn*, that maybe God would prefer you stay home and dive into the crisis that swarms around orphans and widows in your community. It's the real deal.

Plank Versus Sliver

This is a good time to bring up the crux of the matter—self-righteousness. In Matthew 7:3–5, Jesus said,

> Why do you look at the speck of sawdust in your brother's eye and pay no attention to the plank in your own eye? How can you say to your brother, "Let me take the speck out of your eye," when all the time there is a plank in your own eye? You hypocrite, first take the plank out of your own eye, and then you will see clearly to remove the speck from your brother's eye.

The simplest definition of self-righteousness is thinking that your sins are not as bad as someone else's. We've made the Worst Sin List to include the following:

- Sexual immorality of any kind—with homosexuality as the worst of the worst
- Swearing
- Not going to church
- Not tithing
- Voting Democrat
- Listening to Lady Gaga

Yet here's the long list of sins we overlook altogether:

- Divorce and remarriage because of "irreconcilable differences"
- Gossip
- Gluttony
- Lying (of any kind)
- Not loving your neighbor as much as you love yourself
- Not caring for orphans and widows in their distress
- Lawsuits

Regarding the last, 1 Corinthians 6 is explicit that believers should not take legal action against anyone, even if they have been wronged. Yikes!

Consider also God's voice to us at the end of the New Testament in Revelation 3:16 regarding the sin of apathy: "So, because you are lukewarm—neither hot nor cold—I am about to spit you out of my mouth." If there are any words that could be paired like peanut butter and jelly and used to describe the church in America, I think most of us would agree *apathetic* and *lukewarm* probably fit.

Do you see the self-righteousness? We think because we don't swear, watch R-rated movies, or eat without praying, we are better than those who do. Or because our sexual sins are with the opposite sex or they're in our minds while we watch porn, it's not as bad as sexual sins with the same sex. Well, sin is simply missing the mark of God's perfection, so it includes not just *doing* things we shouldn't (aka sins of commission) but also *not doing* all sorts of things Jesus asks us to do (aka sins of omission). Fine, you don't smoke or chew or date girls who do, but how are you doing on loving your neighbor as much as yourself? You don't cheat on your taxes, but are you regularly helping orphans and widows in their distress? You don't watch R-rated movies, but do you give generously and sacrificially to things that matter to God? All the things we do that we are not supposed to do are sins—and all the things we don't do that we *should* do are also sins. It's all missing the mark.

To help you assess your own level of self-righteousness, make a list of sins you commit regularly and then list sins you omit regularly. (I've done this myself—and my level of self-righteousness is higher than I'd like to admit.) For most people who take this seriously, the sins of omission are far more extensive than those committed, but it all counts as not measuring up to the way of Jesus.

Remember, too, that the sins we commit as Christ followers are sins of disobedience rather than the sins of ignorance that most non-believers commit. In other words, we *know* we fall short and choose to continue to do so, which is worse than not knowing you're falling short in the first place.

Gnats Versus Camels

Jesus doesn't mess around with blatant self-righteousness. In Matthew 23:23–24, He said, "You … have neglected the weightier matters of the law: justice and mercy and faithfulness.… You blind guides, straining out a gnat and swallowing a camel!" (ESV).

Obviously sexual issues are a big deal, leading not only to the potentially devastating consequences of unwanted births, abortions, and diseases but also to the possible destruction of families. So it makes sense that throughout history, chastity has been an important trait, especially for someone re-created in Christ. Yet our focus on sexuality has shifted from helping people navigate all the sexual land mines to decrying sexual expression of nearly any kind, especially any sexual orientation apart from one man/one woman. Again, everything that misses God's original intention is sin, but the sins related to homo-sexuality do not pose as great a threat to society as the heterosexual sins we have listed. That is straining gnats but swallowing camels. To date, the issue of gay sex affects less than 5 percent of the population, whereas porn affects more than 80 percent of our culture. And those stats are the same within the church. Which one does the most harm?

In her must-read discussion of sexual orientation and the Christian, *Redeeming Sex: Naked Conversations about Sexuality and*

Spirituality, Debra Hirsch quotes Greg Boyd, author of *Repenting of Religion*, as saying,

> "If we retained a system of evaluating sin at all, sins such as impatience, unkindness, rudeness, and self-righteousness—all indications that love is absent (1 Cor. 13:4–5)—as well as prevalent 'church' sins such as gossip, greed, and apathy would rank higher on our list than sins such as homosexuality or heterosexual promiscuity."

> It seems to me that when we look to Jesus and his assessment of sin, it seems to look very different from the puritan code that prevails in many churches. Where we are tempted to put sexual sin at the top of the pile, Jesus names greed and pride. Money and wealth—not sex—are for Jesus what is most likely to compete with God for our loyalty (Matt. 6:24). Where we are likely to simply expel sexual sinners, Jesus seems to be very merciful and gracious with them (John 8:1–11; John 4:1–26). As much as Jesus cares about the totality of our lives, I sometimes wonder whether Jesus is concerned more by what we do with our money than what we do with our genitals![1]

Debra, in her book *Untamed*, exposes the camels of greed. She cites a study by the World Institute for Development Economics Research at United Nations University, reporting that "the richest 1 percent of adults alone owned 40 percent of all global assets in the year 2000, and that the richest 10 percent of adults accounted for 85 percent of the world total. The bottom half of the world's adult population owned barely 1 percent of all global wealth."[2]

Now, we may think that one greedy individual wouldn't have an impact, but we need to consider that if every Christian repented of greed and chose to live much closer to the simpler ways of Jesus, we Americans alone could probably solve the world's hunger problem (see *Hope Rising: How Christians Can End Extreme Poverty in This Generation* by Scott C. Todd)!

Remember at the beginning of this book we discussed that we should truly avoid false, unfair, or wrong judgment? Good judgment is helpful, but it is time we faced a painful reality. Christian judgment fits exactly into *the categories Jesus challenged the most*, and if the church through the ages had judged people based on what Jesus did, the history of the world would be different. It could still be different.

How it must have shocked the religious establishment of His day to hear Jesus proclaim that the prostitutes and tax collectors would enter the kingdom of God before the Pharisees (Matt. 21:31)! Now we know why. And this knowledge must finally cause us to drop our rocks and feel good about it. Remember, Jesus tossed away the rocks He could have thrown at you. Maybe it's time to drop yours.

What do we know for sure?

- If you sin at all, you have no reason to judge those you don't know.

- If you sin at all, you have no reason to judge those you do know.
- Jesus protected the life of a sinner, and that makes Him an advocate for people who sin.
- Jesus can't stand people who try to catch Him in "the letter of the law" scenarios.
- Jesus was the only person in the adulteress's story who was able to influence her life.
- Jesus was full of grace, and therefore He got a chance to share truth.

What should we change in light of what we know?

- What rocks do you think God might be asking you to drop?
- Is your Christian faith more about sacrifice or mercy? What would it look like if you leaned toward the mercy side?
- What are the planks in your eye? Are you actively and intentionally working on them?
- If Jesus was the most holy and least judgmental, the most righteous and least self-righteous person, what does that mean for you if you claim to follow Him?

Who might this change affect, and what is God asking you to do?

- What gnat have you been trying to strain out of the soup of humanity? Who can you let off the hook, starting tomorrow?

Why is this good news for you?

- Now that you don't have to worry about another person's sliver, you get to use that time to work on your plank.
- This is a great week to simply thank Jesus for applying all of His righteousness to you. You no longer have to be a self-righteous hypocrite.
- This means you can now be a beautifully gentle, humble friend for those who are struggling around you.

4

HINGE POINT: THE WORLD HANGS IN THE BALANCE

The ability to observe without evaluating is
the highest form of intelligence.
—Jiddu Krishnamurti

A story from Warsaw, Ohio, is catching some attention today (August 13, 2014). It seems the dancers at Foxhole nightclub decided to picket a church that had been hassling them for years. Apparently the members and pastor of New Beginnings Ministries felt called by God to try to rid their community of "evil." For nine years, they had been showing up at the club to call the women who worked there terrible names and video the men who entered, threatening to go public with the footage.

Finally the club's employees retaliated. Many of the picketing women were topless as they marched in front of the church. The

owner of the Foxhole, Thomas George, explained why they were
fighting back: "They [the church people] come up every weekend,
and they're very abusive and certainly unchristian-like. Calling the
girls (expletive) and (expletive)." The pastor justified their actions,
saying, "I take very seriously the responsibility as a pastor to see to it
that the gospel of Christ is lifted up … and that evil is confronted."[1]

This may seem like a rather extreme confrontation between the
church and the world, but it brings up important questions about
the tension between our public witness of Jesus and the desire to
make our communities as clean and safe as possible. It brings us
back to where we started: Is there a way for us to stay faithful to
God and our sense of moral obligation without ostracizing, judging,
or coming off as jerks to everyone else? In other words, are we to
force cultural change like conquistadors, or is there another way of
influencing without judging?

When I was living in Portland, I was in an accountability group
with some fellow pastors. One day, we were discussing how much pressure the gay community had been pouring on at the political level to
get legal married status. It had been a hard day, so I was just kicking
back, sipping my latte. But my attempt to chill abruptly ended when
one of the pastors stood up, pounded on the table, and, with neck
veins popping out, said, "We just can't let them win this fight! They
will ruin the holy state of matrimony!" He ran out of breath and sat
down, looking around at us, expecting a standing ovation, I guess.

Nobody said a word, so with the perfect timing of a seasoned
comedian, I said, "Yo, Rev. Here's how I see it: if you really want to
punish the gay community—I mean, if you really want to hit 'em
where it hurts—then let them get married."

Everyone looked at me with scrunched brows, like I had just eaten a cat. "Yeah," I said, "I mean, if you haven't noticed, our little group here started because, Kevin, your wife caught you watching porn, and she's still not sure she can trust you. And, Joe, every week we try to encourage you to not be a complete jerk to Lisa. And, Louie, your wife is constantly telling on you to my wife, especially about how you always prioritize the church over her and the kids. And I'm here because I never seem to find the right balance between work and home so that my kids and Cheryl feel like they are top priority. So, I say let 'em get married, because it is brutal and hard and a daily pain in the neck!"

There was silence for a moment, and then Louie said, "Gosh, I've never thought of that. Seems like we're defiling the sanctity of marriage all the time, eh?" The conversation was much more civilized after that.

Stuck or Embedded?

The key thing to remember here is that being Christian in the world does not mean we're stuck here, simply surviving until we get beamed up. Jesus wants us to be deeply embedded in the muck and mire of humanity without pulling our hair out trying to rid the world of evil. We are here to be salt and light, not judge and jury. As Jesus prayed in John 17:15, specifically for us, "My prayer is not that you take them out of the world but that you protect them from the evil one."

Paul also reminds us in 1 Corinthians 5 that although we don't have to live like the world, we must stay in it.

I wrote to you in my letter not to associate with sexually immoral people—not at all meaning the people of this world who are immoral, or the greedy and swindlers, or idolaters. In that case you would have to leave this world. But now I am writing to you that you must not associate with anyone who claims to be a brother or sister but is sexually immoral or greedy, an idolater or slanderer, a drunkard or swindler. Do not even eat with such people. What business is it of mine to judge those outside the church? Are you not to judge those inside? God will judge those outside. "Expel the wicked person from among you." (vv. 9–13)

We'll talk more about judgment and correction within the community of Jesus followers later, but it's clear that both Jesus and Paul expect us to associate with people "outside the church." It is also reasonable to conclude from Paul's words that to *associate* implies a type of relationship where we are *not* constantly confronting them as they live out their natural lives as unbelievers.

So where is the balance? Is there any hope for living a good, holy life before God while preserving a redemptive relationship with the local pole dancers and topless-bar owners?

Yes, There Is!

In one of Scripture's most poignant stories, some smart aleck's trying to catch Jesus in another religious dilemma:

"Teacher, which is the greatest commandment in the Law?" Jesus replied: "'Love the Lord your God with all your heart and with all your soul and with all your mind.' This is the first and greatest commandment. And the second is like it: 'Love your neighbor as yourself.' All the Law and the Prophets hang on these two commandments." (Matt. 22:36–40)

Wow, *all* the Law and the Prophets? Do you know how astonishing that thought would have been to His listeners? That's tantamount to saying that everything you've ever heard or read about God in the Old Testament hangs on these two simple ideas. Everything on which you base your devotion, every theological point you hold dear, every single issue of personal holiness you are trying to faithfully live out—everything literally and figuratively hinges on these two simple commandments! What a mind-boggling simplification of a religious system that seems so intricate, confusing, and contradictory to people.

It's easy to look down on the jerk who asked Jesus this question. But we're not even halfway through this book, and already we've read scriptures that, taken by themselves, would give anyone the impression that we *should* judge people, we *should* challenge our culture, we *should* confront sin all the time. In fact, as I was studying every passage on judgment to prepare to write *Brimstone*, I kept getting mad at God, thinking, *Sheesh, it's no wonder we can't figure it out. No wonder so many feel "called" to stand on the street corner with a megaphone. No wonder we're so harsh with each other as Christians. Didn't You see this coming?*

So maybe the guy asking Jesus this question wasn't trying to trick Him after all. Maybe he was like us—simply trying to make sense of his entire religious system. He needed something solid to hang on to.

Being from Colorado, I'm learning a few things about rock climbing. Some jargon climbers use for handholds are buckets and crimps. Crimps are small crevices or indentations in a rock into which you can just barely get the ends of your fingers (usually the last joint) or toes. Buckets are just what they sound like—they are big, easy-to-grab holds from which you can dangle or even set your bed and equipment on to sleep for the night.

To love God with all you've got and also love your neighbor as much as you love yourself (which is a lot)—that's a bucket hold! In this verse, Jesus is not blowing off every scripture and tradition His followers had learned. He's just summarizing all the apparently contradictory scriptures into one big idea, into a larger truth. And this is really important when trying to understand the true nature of judgment, as well as many other issues in Scripture that seem harsh on their own.

Okay, so back to our bucket hold. Here Jesus is giving us the key to living a holy life while successfully influencing people around us. Another way to say this is that Jesus has given us His personal key that unlocks how to be full of grace and full of truth all at the same time.

"Love the Lord your God with all your heart, mind, soul, and strength" is Jesus's way of saying, "Hey, you get to live any way you want toward Me. You get to do everything—marriage, money, morality, life—as you believe you should. You get to parent your kids the way you want, you get to choose what you want to eat and drink, how you want to spend your Sabbath, what you'll do with extra money, whatever. It doesn't matter what other people decide to do with all these issues. No other person's choices, orientations, philosophies, or idiosyncrasies will determine what's right or wrong for you. Even if everyone defiles the sanctity of marriage and the sanctity of life around you, you don't have to. You can still serve God. It's like Joshua said: 'As for me and my house, we will serve the Lord.' If the government someday chooses to legalize concubines or polygamy, you still get to choose one spouse. If they legalize all kinds of crazy drugs, you don't have to smoke, snort, inject, or topically apply them.

"So relax, chill out, and be happy that you don't have to freak out or fight against every social abnormality.

"ANNNNDDDDDD …

"You have to love the jokers next to you, which means you cannot force the way you live unto Me (vertically) onto anyone else (horizontally). You have to love the guy married to three women. You have to love the twenty-year-old who has three kids out of wedlock. You have to love the Islamic man whose call-to-prayer siren wakes you up every morning at four o'clock in the morning. You have to love the five fraternity boys who create thick fog banks of pot smoke that waft into your kitchen window and put your children down for an early nap. They don't live like you, they don't like what you like, they don't worship Me as you do, but I want you to love them. And, yes, that means you shouldn't hassle the topless pole dancers."

First Peter 3:15–16 confirms this balance:

> But in your hearts revere Christ as Lord. Always be
> prepared to give an answer to everyone who asks
> you to give the reason for the hope that you have.
> But do this with gentleness and respect, keeping

a clear conscience, so that those who speak mali-
ciously against your good behavior in Christ may
be ashamed of their slander.

Where do we revere Christ? In our hearts! Not in the media or
on Facebook or in a forced, aggressive conversation with said sinner.
Again, you get to live as you know Jesus wants you to, *and* you don't
need to worry about judging others. According to this, it is the living
witness of our vertical relationship with God that will eventually win
the day with those neighbors we'd just as soon shoot as love. This
is why the pastor and his parishioners got it terribly wrong. They
think "lifting up the gospel of Christ" to the culture means fighting
against every perceived evil. But the gospel of Jesus is about gentle
persuasion through respected friendships, not violent confrontation
with enemies.

This is what we can call a hinge point. Everything hinges upon
us living this balance of vertical personal commitment to Jesus without imposing horizontally upon the humans around us.

Neighbors

So what about these neighbors Jesus makes such a big deal about?
Remember, all the Law and the Prophets hinge on your ability and
willingness to love these people. Neighbors are not acquaintances
or drive-by nameless humans. They are also not family, nor are they
friends, initially. Neighbors represent a unique type of relationship
that must be intentionally pursued and nurtured just like anyone
else you would someday hope to love. This is why Jesus puts so much

emphasis on those who live right next door. And make no mistake, Jesus knew exactly what He was doing.

In summary, neighbors make real Christians out of us. It's a relationship you don't have to pursue, and most will think you're weird if you do, but if we take Jesus at His word, this one command can change any neighborhood almost overnight.

So here are a few pointers to help you as you move forward.

First, neighbors aren't thinking about how to love you. This is not a two-way street. You've got to be the one to initiate contact and then continue to initiate contact, and the only thing you should be trying to do with your neighbors is to get their stories and make friends. Remember that Jesus was called a friend of sinners, which means that although He lived in a way that was miles more holy than they did, He still tucked His moral superiority under His tunic and spent consistent time after work, on weekends, and in early mornings getting to know people at the heart level. So no matter what Google reveals about your neighbors or what you've heard them scream at their kids or spouses through open windows, you must not make any judgments early on.

In the Halter family story, we've had many neighbors find faith in Christ and eventually make their way into our churches, but every one of these required twenty to thirty dinners, happy hours, golf outings, and poker nights to get a real picture of who they were.

Second, neighbors are sojourners. That is, they are just traveling through. Chances are most of the people next door to you have not always lived there. In Denver proper and the surrounding suburbs, people move, on average, every eighteen months. That means they are most likely going to be from another part of the

country or world where they have strange customs, skin colors that
don't match yours, different religions, and different forms of sexual
orientation. Many will like a glass of wine with dinner, and in states
like Colorado, they may even light up a joint in the backyard to
help them relax while their kids are playing with your kids out
in the tree house. Some will overwater their yard, some will not
water at all and instead grow a wheat field, and most will not heed
neighborhood covenants. If you're from a town like Portland, your
neighbor to the right may park his semitruck in the front yard and
eclipse your home (should the sun happen to come out). The guy
(or maybe the gal ... you don't know yet which the transsexual
identifies as) to your left may have a chicken coop and organic
garden that reek of chicken poop. A Mongolian family of twenty-
eight may live across the street, and the rough-and-tumble Mafia
guy who likes to get in fights once a year in the middle of the street
may be kitty-corner to you.

These actually were my neighbors in Oregon! Trust me, with
neighbors like these, you'll want to judge and avoid everyone!

But you can't do that because you follow Jesus, and Jesus can't
wait for you to meet them, serve them, enjoy their company, and
find ways to love them. To do this you've got to let them be themselves so that when the Holy Spirit begins to convict them of sin,
righteousness, and holiness, your self-righteousness won't have got-
ten in the way.

In his book *The Cost of Discipleship*, Dietrich Bonhoeffer high-
lights Jesus as mediator—the one who stands between God and
humans. But he expands the mediatory role of Jesus beyond being
simply between humans and God, saying,

We learn that in the most intimate relationships of life, in our kinship with father and mother, brothers and sisters, in married love, and in our duty to the community, direct relationships are impossible. Since the coming of Christ, his followers have no more immediate realities of their own, not in their family relationships nor in the ties with their nation nor in the relationships formed in the process of living. Between father and son, husband and wife, the individual and the nation, stands Christ the Mediator, whether they are able to recognize him or not. We cannot establish direct contact outside ourselves except through him, through his word, and through our following of him. To think otherwise is to deceive ourselves....

There is no way from one person to another. However loving and sympathetic we try to be, however sound our psychology, however frank and open our behaviour, we cannot penetrate the incognito of the other man [or woman] for there are no direct relationships, not even between soul and soul. Christ stands between us, and we can only get into touch with our neighbours through him.[2]

The Greatest Sin

As with most parables or stories of Jesus, we are supposed to process this one from all angles. So to say that the greatest commandment is to love God with everything you've got and to love your neighbors as much as you love yourself also means that the greatest sin may be to love God haphazardly, only on weekends, or only when you need something from Him, while at the same time having no real interest in caring for, loving on, doing a barbeque with, or even getting to know the names of your neighbors.

Isn't it amazing how we've made swearing, having sex before marriage, watching R-rated movies, and having a beer with dinner and a joint for dessert seem like sins damnable by the eternal fires of hell, but we continue to ignore Jesus's statement on the greatest commandments and greatest sins?

A Little Pointer on Keeping a Balance

Here's a little bonus tip that I've found helpful to keep my wits about me as I live next to these wild Vikings we call sinners, pagans, and wacko unbelievers while keeping my vertical relationship with God strong. It's called "whimsical holiness," which is the ability to hold on to personal values of Christlikeness while being deeply in relationship with people who do not hold your same convictions. In other words, it's about keeping a sense of humor while keeping a sense of holiness.

Looking again to Jesus, I think we can agree that He was holy. But whimsical? Sure. When Jesus made more wine than an elephant could suck down, for people who were already hammered drunk, it was a whimsical decision. When Jesus sneaked up behind the two men walking to Emmaus, He must have had a smirk on His face. When He held a dinner for every despicable tax collector in town, He must have had to crack a few opening jokes to help them relax. When He was talking about spiritual truth with the confused woman at the well, He responded with gracious statements instead of belittling her or straightening out her poor theology. When He purposefully neglected to remind His disciples to wash their hands correctly before eating, He was also being whimsically holy. Heck, eating and drinking were His pastime. My favorite scripture, Luke 7:34, says it this way: "The Son of Man came eating and drinking, and you say, 'Here is a glutton and a drunkard, a friend of tax collectors and sinners.'"

And, yes, while Jesus was with all these people who were doing all these sinful things, He was holy. Like a veteran social worker on Skid Row who has seen it all and knows the backstory behind the brokenness, He deals with the whole person, not just the observable sinful patterns. Like a wise judge with years behind the bench, He's able to cut through the BS and get to the heart of the matter. Like a middle linebacker who effortlessly shunts aside three-hundred-pound offenders coming at Him so He can get to the quarterback, Jesus shunts off sins to win the heart of the sinner.

God has been to the brothels, the bars, and the back alleys of Sin City. People with Jesus's whimsical holiness don't gasp when someone curses. They don't avoid a group of people, a place, or a party because someone might get out of hand. They inhabit dark places with the intention of protecting and redeeming, befriending and befuddling people with acceptance and love. They win the lost because they're the only ones who hang out with the lost.

This is the power of incarnation (living our human life like Jesus lived His) and the character of whimsical holiness with which every Christian must learn to clothe him- or herself. Redemption, liberation, and sanctification are dirty jobs. The dirtiest! And to follow Christ is to jump into pain, hell, and all kinds of sinful acts without an arrogant, finger-pointing, judgmental thought.

What do we know for sure?

- We don't influence culture by yelling at it.
- Confronting sin without first influencing the heart creates more space between us and them.
- We never have to fear what the culture calls acceptable because we are always free to love God with all our heart, mind, soul, and strength. You are safe and free!
- We should never impose our vertical moral commitments to God upon the horizontal plane of relationships, especially our neighbors.

What should we change in light of what we know?

- We should put away or put down any aggressive tactics of forcing people to live as we do. We can vote, but that's about it.
- We should reopen or initiate friendship with people around us regardless of our differences.

Who might this change affect, and what is God asking you to do?

- You can't love your neighbors unless you at least know their names. How can you find out the names of each of your neighbors and their children without freaking people out? Plan that for this month.

How is this good news for you?

- All you have to do vertically is revere Christ in your heart.
- All you have to do horizontally is not become a stumbling block to what Jesus is trying to create between you and them.

5

MISSING-OLOGY: NONJUDGMENT 401

How easy it is to judge rightly after one sees
what evil comes from judging wrongly.
—Elizabeth Gaskell, *Wives and Daughters*

A few months back I was speaking at a conference in Australia, a country that is known for being a primarily secular culture. The people are honest and sacrilegious, and I assumed the church folks would be pretty open to my thoughts regarding living in the world like Jesus did. But after one of my talks, I was cornered by two lovely middle-aged lasses who said, "Mr. Hugh, can we share a concern we have with what you're telling everyone?" Before I could say anything, they jumped right in: "I don't think you should mention that you take yoga classes in a public Christian setting. I think it's going to lead a lot of people into danger."

Curious, I said, "What could be dangerous about yoga, other than pulling a hammy or dislocating your face or something?"

Not catching my joke, one of them said, "Well, you know, yoga is based in other spiritualism, and if you go to a class you are opening yourself up to all sorts of evil and demonic influences."

"Hmmm, well, ma'am, I have heard of this type of thinking, but can you tell me where in the Bible you think it says that we should be afraid of other religions or people who practice other religions?" They both just stared at me with twisted faces, like when you eat Vegemite for the very first time. I continued, "And if what you're saying is true—that we can pick up a demon here or there like a common flu virus—don't you think it's going to be a bit hard to influence them with the gospel of Jesus?"

The conversation ended cordially, but I had the distinct impression that no matter what I showed them scripturally or argued logically, the real world was something to be afraid of and avoided instead of engaged in, at least in their ironclad theology.

Adventures in Missing the Point

As we have hopefully settled some issues on judgment, I think it would be good to take a hard left turn and let you know that judgment really isn't the big issue in this book. The real issue is that judgment keeps us from the Big Deal, the Main Point, which is to live out our true missionary calling.

You've probably heard the old Christian slogan "Be in the world, but not of it." I understand that in rubbing against humanity we are not to take on the ways of the world, that of course there are dangers inherent in street life. But I have to push back a bit here and ask: *Hasn't our fear of the world produced the opposite effect? Aren't we Christians more of the world these days and also not really in it?*

Let's take another look at the passage this slogan comes from:

> I have given them your word, and the world has hated them because they are not of the world, just as I am not of the world. I do not ask that you take them out of the world, but that you keep them from the evil one. They are not of the world, just as I am not of the world. Sanctify them in the truth; your word is truth. As you sent me into the world, so I have sent them into the world. And for their sake I consecrate myself, that they also may be sanctified in truth. (John 17:14–19 ESV)

I'm not sure I even caught this the first hundred times I read it, but Jesus is showing us that once we are in Christ, something happens that we cannot see. Before, we were of the world, but in Christ, we are no longer of the world. Jesus says about His own disciples, "They are not of the world any more than I am of the world" (NIV). Clearly this doesn't mean they had left the actual physical world, so it must mean that in the unseen realm only God sees, we have a spiritual change of position.

Paul talked about other positional changes that happen in the invisible realm when he said that we are crucified with Christ, that we are seated in the heavenly realms. In other words, when we put our faith in Jesus, many things happen to us in the spiritual realm that we may not see in the physical. The biggest change is that we become citizens of another country—the kingdom of God. This world is no longer our home, and the rest of our Christian experience is about learning how to live for another land.

So when Jesus asks His Father not to take us out of the world, He's not asking for God to leave us here spiritually, but physically and emotionally. It's as if Jesus takes us to heaven when our soul is converted, but He sends us back so we can accomplish the mission He has for us. He doesn't ask us whether or not we want to go back, He just does it. Jesus is King, after all, and what He wants is not something we can opt out of. It's not something He reserves for only the Christian superstars. Being sent is part and parcel of being in the family of God—He wants us to be on mission with Him. It's an aspect of our new identity. We are redeemed and then sent back as missionary saints.

I suspect Jesus knows that when we abstain from the world, we actually become more susceptible to spiritual sickness. It's like the moms and dads who splash antiseptic gel all over their kids every five minutes to make sure they never catch a bug, only to discover that their kids get sick more often because their bodies haven't developed the natural immunity that comes from exposure to viruses and bacteria. I think Jesus wants to keep us in the world because it's great for the world *and* it's good for us.

Remember that Jesus exposed His disciples to demons. He had them go places where they would get hurt. He, unlike any other rabbi or Jewish man, had close female friends, and some of these women were known for their sexual past. Jesus took His followers into violent neighborhoods, and rather than taking the boys to synagogue on the Sabbath, He took them to the homes of pagans, prostitutes, professional publicans, and money-grubbers. Yes, Jesus was training them so they would know how to live like Him, but He also was strengthening their missionary muscles.

Missiology 101

Circling back around, I hope you are starting to see why I'm saying that nonjudgment or removing lousy judgment is not the goal of this book. But I'm spending so much time on it here because it is a major issue that clearly keeps us, God's people, from living out our calling to be agents of good news in this world. You may have learned in church (ecclesiology) that you should be afraid of the world, that you should avoid it and protect your kids from it. But missiology and the story of God teaches us that rather than fearing the world, we should instead change it, that greater is He that is within us than he that is in the world. Therefore to help people out of false religions or empty hopes, or simply to position your life to be available, you just might have to roll out a yoga mat, develop a taste for merlot, join a local beer league softball team, or volunteer some time in the hood.

Okay, wait, what's this missiology thing?

In layman's terms, missiology is the study of how to bring the gospel to the world. Not just the rhetoric of the gospel but the visible, tangible reality of God's kingdom here on earth. *Missiology* comes from God, the *Missio Dei* (mission of God). The words *mission* or *missional* actually mean "to be sent," so missiology is the study, or really the story, of how God comes to us, sends His Son to help us, and especially what it means when Jesus tells us, "As the Father has sent me, I am sending you" (John 20:21).

To get a bit more technical, missiology combines the study of God (theology) with the study of man (anthropology). Anthropology studies languages, religions, cultural dynamics, and history. In other words, to be a good missionary, you can't just go "preach the Word" and spew Bible verses left and right, or try to scare people from hell or their sin. That is what I call "missing-ology." You've got to understand all the unique nuances of human social interaction, biases, and psychology, or, in missions terminology, what is the "context" within which the humans you hope to influence live.

If you are doing missing-ology, you are minimizing almost everything that makes people human beings. You are making blanket statements, generalizing, stereotyping, and simplifying a complex problem down to a Bible verse. In short, you are judging them. And this just doesn't work because it is not the way of Jesus, who entered people's grungy lives in order to make them whole—to make them *more* human.

Missing-ology 101

I once heard about missionaries in the Congo preaching from the riverbank and calling for commitments from the Congolese to submit to baptism with no success. They berated the people for their lack of devotion. Later they found out that the Congolese knew the river was crawling with man-eating crocs. Uhhh, duh!

Or what about the missionaries preaching in Africa from Revelation 3:20 (ESV), "Behold, I stand at the door and knock," without knowing that in this African context only thieves knock on doors to see if anyone is home. Friends, on the other hand, announce their presence by calling out. So these missionaries were inadvertently preaching that Jesus wanted to steal from them!

In recent times, you may have heard about members of the infamous Westboro Baptist Church moving beyond merely picketing homosexuals and returning war veterans, and showing up in Iraq to tell the Islamists they will burn in hell.

Personally, I've coached missionaries from all over the world and I've seen the same miscues. I've met American missionaries in Ireland who wanted to influence the city folk, yet they chose to live thirty minutes out in the countryside. And they didn't drink beer. I'm not saying every Irishman drinks a pint of Guinness, but if you plan on reaching more than the two people who don't, you may need to develop a taste for it or pick another country to missionize.

Some of these stories are funny, but in reality it's painful to hear how God's people have missed so many missional opportunities because we lead out with Bible verses or invitations to come back to our church services instead of leading out with listening, learning, and loving. Where did all this bad missional behavior come from? Take a deep breath with me … I think it came from the Bible. This may seem like a deep rabbit hole to go down, but we really can't be effective in God's mission unless we deal with how we approach the Holy Scriptures. Consider this basic training—part of being a citizen of God's kingdom.

Bible Blunders 101

The Bible is not a collection of sayings or a litany of Bible verses. It is a missionary training manual. The biblical narrative is a cohesive story that tells us how God came to us, what He did for us, and how He sends us as missionaries to the world. The New Testament letters have been written, preserved, and overseen by the Spirit of God and faithfully handed down to a community of missionary saints who are on the move, in the trenches, and under duress. So the first adjustment we must consider is that the Bible is not a spiritual formation guide for missionless sermon-mongers. It does not call you to holiness without calling you to hang with the world at the exact same time.

We must also remember that to fully understand any story we have to have a good grasp of the context in which it was written. As with all Eastern literature, the Bible was written within and for an entirely Eastern context over thousands of years, so our interpretation as Westerners will naturally be skewed simply because we don't see things through an Eastern lens. Easterners are more interpretational. Westerners take things at face value—we find it more comfortable to take things literally. This one reason alone is why we use Scripture to beat people up. There are lots of one-liners, and if we don't force ourselves to speak the words of God in full context of the larger story, we'll almost always force judgment upon people.

Easterners look through the words as if through a pool of water for deeper, subversive, and more abstruse meanings. Westerners see only surface meanings, what's right in front of their faces, and therefore struggle to accept paradox and mystery. Easterners view stories and statements from multiple angles and assume paradox and mystery. This may sound scary to someone from a Western culture because we don't like multiple meanings—but Jesus was well versed in subversive meanings, and we have to learn to give a little space for two people to get something a little different from one Bible verse. Westerners need to have immediate resolution, and we're comfortable only if everything makes sense. We like to systematize doctrine and theology so we can have answers for every situation, just like the religious leaders in Jesus's day who had determined the cause of that man's blindness to be someone's sin ("Who sinned, this man or his parents?"). So we, too, try to explain through our systematic theology why someone is gay, or how someone with a certain political orientation can't be a solid Christian, or why God allowed an earthquake to wipe out whole towns in Haiti.

This is a critical point—our Christian faith started in a purely Eastern context, so it will be impossible to learn the missional ways of Jesus if we don't learn to read and interpret the Bible through an Eastern lens. How can we get better at this? Learn the *whole* of Scripture instead of just points of Scripture.

Watch Out for Lists

One of the main reasons we jump to judgment is because of lists in the Bible.

For instance, in 1 Timothy Paul is encouraging a young pastor, Timothy, from wasting his time arguing over scriptures and myths or traditions that others were holding on to. In 1:5–17 Paul says,

> The goal of this command is love, which comes
> from a pure heart and a good conscience and a
> sincere faith. Some have departed from these and
> have turned to meaningless talk. They want to be

teachers of the law, but they do not know what they are talking about or what they so confidently affirm.

We know that the law is good if one uses it properly. We also know that the law is made not for the righteous but for lawbreakers and rebels, the ungodly and sinful, the unholy and irreligious, for those who kill their fathers or mothers, for murderers, for the sexually immoral, for those practicing homosexuality, for slave traders and liars and perjurers—and for whatever else is contrary to the sound doctrine that conforms to the gospel concerning the glory of the blessed God, which he entrusted to me.

I thank Christ Jesus our Lord, who has given me strength, that he considered me trustworthy, appointing me to his service. Even though I was once a blasphemer and a persecutor and a violent man, I was shown mercy because I acted in ignorance and unbelief. The grace of our Lord was poured out on me abundantly, along with the faith and love that are in Christ Jesus.

Here is a trustworthy saying that deserves full acceptance: Christ Jesus came into the world to save sinners—of whom I am the worst. But for that very reason I was shown mercy so that in me, the worst of sinners, Christ Jesus might display his immense patience as an example for those who would believe in him and receive eternal life. Now

to the King eternal, immortal, invisible, the only
God, be honor and glory for ever and ever. Amen.

Now, when you read this, what do you focus on? My guess is that
you focused on homosexuality, right? It's natural whenever sins are
listed back to back to start comparing, contrasting, and construct-
ing an argument against people, especially when something you are
struggling with is mentioned. Lists just do that to people. They give
us the justification to say, "See, it's right there! There's no way to
argue against it!"

Yet in this passage Paul brings up several key points that actually
point us against judgment.

For instance, he is warning Timothy about believers who are
getting lost in futile arguments. Their arguments appear to be
about the Law of Moses, which means these people were using the
Law to judge people harshly. Paul says here that the Law must be
used properly, implying that it is still helpful in exposing patterns
of behavior that are not representative of God's original design. So
Paul's listing of homosexuality among other sins is honest, but it
doesn't necessarily follow that we are to use lists to judge people.
The list is there to inform us of God's design, but Paul starts and
ends this section with love, and the challenge is to avoid arguments
and use the list appropriately. So when you see a list of sins, you
may think it is evidence that we should use the Law against those
sinners and that when we tell them their lives don't measure up it
will draw them to Jesus. But it's the opposite. Paul knows and has
already written much to the church about how none are righteous
and that all have sinned and fit the list. This is why he then tells

his own story of how he was the "worst of sinners," exposing how gracious God was to come to him and call him to ministry. So lists are helpful and useful in helping us see that we are all sinners, but they are not to be used to judge others.

Does this mean that we never bring up our failures and sin? Does it mean we, as friends of normal people, never discuss or bring up ideas of how to live better? Of course not. All Paul is showing is that if we put ourselves in the list and if we openly discuss our own sin, it will be easier to have these discussions without any sense of elite judgmentalism.

Why does this matter? Because we've been bad missionaries and have lost our credibility, our ability to impact people, through mishandling the Word of truth. It's time to get more serious about reading, understanding, and interpreting God's heart through His revealed Word.

Bad Words

So here are a couple of words we've got to rethink.

The first one people often misuse and abuse when trying to argue a point is the word *biblical*. For example, someone might say, "We plan on having a biblical marriage," or "Homosexuality is not biblical," or "That was a really biblical sermon." Look, anything in the Bible is biblical, since the meaning of *biblical* is anything that comes from the Bible! So using the term this way not only sounds arrogant but also is completely unhelpful.

A professional golfer and outspoken Christian was once asked by reporters about his faith and how people viewed him. He said, "I just try to live my life by the Bible and live a biblical life." We all get what he meant, but a person really can't live by the Bible. We can let the story of the Bible inform how we live, but there are many lifestyle options in the Bible we might find unsavory. You could live biblically by taking one thousand wives, like Solomon did. Or stoning your rebellious children to death, as the Law requires. Or owning slaves, like Paul's good pal, and returning runaway slaves to their masters, as Paul did himself.

I remember once getting upset that my teenage daughter didn't want to go to church—the one I was pastoring—and while pouting, I told my wife, "It's just not biblical that a pastor's daughter doesn't want to go to church." My wife, cutting through the BS, held up her quote fingers and said, "It's also not 'biblical' that your daughter grows to resent the church or that her dad cares more about what other people might think than what is really going on in his daughter's heart." Touché. I stopped pouting. Kind of.

Another misused word that makes judgment really easy is *literal*. Literalism means that you take what you hear or read literally, at face value, without any concern for the overall teaching or context of the subject in question. For instance, while I was in seminary, people would fight over which translation of the Bible was a more literal translation. What they were shooting for was the closest possible version to the original text, thinking if they had the most literal words they would get at truth faster. I was on this bandwagon myself, but what I'm now learning is that Jesus doesn't want us to be literal or to care about which translation gets you closer to the original wording. He wants us to use our brains and look at the totality of teaching on any issue, consider the historical and social context in which it was written, put a little Eastern hat on (maybe a fez?), and then process the true meanings behind what we're reading.

The version is not the issue; the truth and living out of the truth is the issue. That's why Jesus says in John 5:39–40, "You study the Scriptures diligently because you think that in them you have eternal life. These are the very Scriptures that testify about me, yet you refuse to come to me to have life." Jesus isn't nearly as amped up that you can parse phrases or cross-reference verses as He is about your ability and willingness to cross cultures and represent Him well. As with all Eastern thought, Jesus and Paul taught that "knowledge puffs up while love builds up" (1 Cor. 8:1).

If we took every sentence literally, women would have to cover their heads with doilies and never talk in church. Men would all be blind and have no limbs or reproductive organs because Jesus said, "If your right eye causes you to stumble, gouge it out and throw it away.… And if your right hand causes you to stumble, cut it off and throw it away" (Matt. 5:29–30). If we were literal, most rich people could not be a part of our churches, since "it is easier for a camel to go through the eye of a needle than for someone who is rich to enter the kingdom of God" (Matt. 19:24). Words or phrases like being *born again* or *crucified with Christ* would also send us into a tailspin. If we were really serious about literal interpretation, Christians would also not get so nervous about supernatural experiences with demons, healings, selling all your possessions, or martyrdom, since these things seem pretty standard for Jesus and His early followers.

Remember, different books of the Bible were written in different literary genres. Some are more historical in orientation, some are more didactic or oriented toward teaching, and some books, like Revelation, are deeply metaphorical, with almost every sentence couched in startling and confusing imagery. Some are songs and poems, like the Song of Solomon. Heck, if you literally lived out this book, Christians would be known more for lurid sexual exploits than chastity. Popular song lyrics like "Really love your peaches, wanna shake your tree," would become slogans our kids would wear on their T-shirts to proselytize at school! (Sorry to co-opt your song, Steve Miller Band!) Seriously, the Song of Solomon is a much more erotic read than Steve Miller's song.

Even the word *wrath* should be handled better. The word simply means "passionate displeasure." Can you imagine what your kids would think of you if you wedged *wrath* into your tirade every time you were angry with them? "Joey, if you track in mud one more time, I will bring my wrath down upon you!" Yikes.

But it wouldn't be so bad if you said, "I'm just passionate about your life and nothing hurts me more than when you hurt yourself, so I'm just really displeased with the choices you are making right now." You can see the power of words. But because some translators decided to use the word *wrath*, we take it to mean an avalanche of holy terror will come down on deserving godless heathens and heretical teachers, rather than meaning that God feels angry and disappointed over watching sin tear His children apart.

Again, I'm not bringing this up to dissuade you from having a strong interest in truth or the Bible. I'm actually challenging us all, myself included, to have a much higher view of truth and the Bible than most of us currently have. When we isolate scripture, we isolate people. When we are prepared to fight rather than love, we use words as ammo and the Bible as a weapon. When we pick the verses we like and overlook the ones we don't, we make God in our likeness rather than growing more fully into His. As Voltaire famously said, "If God has made us in his image, we have returned him the favor."

Look, we can't blame the Bible for our pervasive judgmental posture toward people. We must blame ourselves for reading it poorly and using it selfishly.

The Good Word

So is there a word we should use when thinking of the Bible? How about *authoritative*?

Saying the Bible is authoritative means that we can trust it and that we, by faith, bank on the character and power of God to hand down to us a good enough chunk of literature by which to piece together the story of God and the story of man. Authority of Scripture means that we can learn from it, apply it, and position it above our own wisdom and opinions. It also means its authority doesn't come from us, from the fact that we call it the Bible. Its authority comes from God. I once heard a story in which biblical scholar N. T. Wright was asked if there was anything more authoritative to him than the Bible. His answer was, "Of course, for sure." To the shocked crowd, he said, "*God* is more authoritative."

God formed the universe out of nothing and created every living creature—for starters. So wouldn't there be more about Himself than He could ever put in one book? And of course Jesus was there at creation—"Through him all things were made; without him nothing was made that has been made" (John 1:3)—and He is the image of the invisible God, so Jesus is also more authoritative than the Bible.

Look, I'm not playing games with you to frustrate you, but I need to say this so you change the way you talk out there. If you say, "Well, the Bible says _____," to try to make a point about behavior or to gain the upper hand in a conversation with your neighbor, guess what? Nobody gives a rip. Your neighbors won't recognize the Bible's authority because they don't believe in it. It is authoritative for those who do believe in it and align their lives according to the grand story within its pages. Peter, by his reading of Old Testament Scripture, was sure that salvation could be only for the Jewish people. Until Jesus gave him a mystical dream to expose a higher authority than his book. In the same way, Jesus showed up and blew one of the most learned Pharisees of His time away with power, and eventually Paul let Jesus be more authoritative than all his scriptural knowledge. In my own life I've had seismic shifts in understanding certain scriptures, and now I'm ashamed and have to laugh about how I've made an idol out of the Bible instead of humbling myself under Jesus and His Scriptures.

Pulling It All Together

In summary, our interpretation of the Bible is not authoritative. We must somehow accept that, in the Scriptures, we have writings that help us find God, who is the authority. The Bible should humble us, not puff us up. It should be something we treat as precious and serious, rather than something that leads us to quick judgments that we use to control people. N. T. Wright said,

Authority is not the power to control people, and crush them, and keep them in little boxes. The church often tries to do that—to tidy people up. Nor is the Bible as the vehicle of God's authority meant to be information for the legalist.... God's authority vested in scripture is designed, as all God's authority is designed, to liberate human beings, to judge and condemn evil and sin in the world in order to set people free to be fully human. That's what God is in the business of doing.[1]

What do we know for sure?

- God and Jesus are more authoritative than the Bible.
- The Bible is written to missionary saints who are sent into the world.
- God doesn't want us to be afraid of the world.
- Every Bible verse must be handled in context of the larger story of God, not picked apart to prove our points.
- It is okay that people interpret passages of Scripture differently.

What should we change in light of what we know?

- We should take the Word of God more seriously.

- We are better off to interpret Scripture in community and learn how to listen to God's unique voice in different ways and in different meanings.
- We should become better listeners, and when we are uncomfortable, we should trust God to reveal Himself over time instead of at the end of every small-group study or sermon.

Who might this change affect, and what is God asking you to do?

- If we viewed our small group, Bible study group, or home community as a group of people who are learning the larger story of God together, maybe a few other people would fit in. Consider doing away with invitations to your church or to Bible studies and instead invite people to come "talk about life and God and pray for each other." I think you'll find people are much more open when the reason we gather is more open-minded.

Why is this good news for you?

- Your job isn't to end every conversation with "truth"; instead, it is to keep the conversation running.

- You can trust God to reveal Himself over time as you keep learning Scripture together.
- You will grow because you no longer view your beliefs as right but stay postured as a learner and a child before Jesus every day.

6

STREET-LEVEL SAINTS

Unity in essentials, liberty in nonessentials, charity in all things.
—The Puritans

Now that we've taken a good chunk of time to discuss some important nuances that are critical to living as a representative of Jesus, let's get down on the street level a bit where the real stuff happens.

Jesus is the way, the truth, and the life, so clearly truth is important to Him. But for Jesus, truth isn't abstract truth. It isn't just information or concepts to consider. For Jesus truth is Him: His ways, His reality offered to people. As such, Jesus cares most about our response to truth and the level at which it is accepted, received, or followed. In other words, a follower of Jesus should be as concerned about helping people want to come toward the truth as he is about the truth itself. Another way to say it is that our missionary call is about creating an atmosphere in which people are drawn to the truth, come to respect the person in which truth is found, and accept the truth personally. This applies to those who are not yet followers of Jesus, as well as we who already believe but who may have some incorrect theology.

For example, you may be correct on the scripture that says God hates divorce, but when you're trying to "be there" for someone going through a divorce or someone who has already been divorced, Jesus wants you to get beyond the point of that *scripture* and help your friend move toward the person behind the point. That is, *Him*. Until someone is in a place to respond, realign, reevaluate, or repent toward Jesus, the points fall flat.

Let's say your neighbor Sally asks you if she can sleep on your couch for a few days until the divorce proceedings are finished, and you say, "You are welcome to stay here, Sally, but I need to know that you are aware that Jesus hates divorce, and I'm not comfortable in helping you unless I know you've done all you can to make it work."

How do you think Sally would feel?

Judged, at the *very* least. Offered unconditional love? Probably not. My guess is that on the street level, the end result would not be as Jesus wanted. In accordance with truth or trying to win people's openness to truth, consider if Sally was offered a free place to stay for as long as it helped. And what if you, as Sally's friend, committed to pray for her often, encourage her, and be there to listen and speak gentle words of hope and wisdom? My guess is that more of the truth would be received, and quite possibly Sally would continue to bounce off of and respond to the person of Jesus.

Being the Truth Is Better Than Imposing the Truth

As we take concepts and flesh them out on the street, let's look at a verse many use to justify overaggressive confrontation. First Timothy 3:15 tells us we must behave "in God's household, which is the church of the living God, the pillar and foundation of the truth." This verse, if interpreted poorly, gives people the impression that we are to teach truth, defend it, and protect it as if it were a corruptible treasure. Thus many Christians try to stand up or argue for truth. But this is not the meaning. To be a pillar or foundation means to be a support or an example of. And where is this to happen? According to this, it should happen within the church itself. In other words, we are to be the truth and live the truth inside the family of God, but also in plain view of onlookers who watch us live out our truth. The responsibility is on us in the church to live the truth long before we go public, get political, or pound the pulpit in defense of the truth. The finger should be pointed at us, not at those who have not yet put their faith in Jesus.

First Corinthians 5:11–12 speaks to this, and it is actually a very hard verse as it talks about disassociating with some people.

> But now I am writing to you that you must not
> associate with anyone who claims to be a brother or
> sister but is sexually immoral or greedy, an idolater
> or slanderer, a drunkard or swindler. Do not even
> eat with such people. What business is it of mine
> to judge those outside the church? Are you not to
> judge those inside?

Again, as we talked about in chapter 4 (Hinge Point), truth is viable only inside a community of people who accept it. I know that truth is true everywhere, like fire's ability to burn you in a brothel as easily as in a church. But truth can help a person only if he is willing to submit his life to it. And since the church is made of people who are learning to realign their lives under the reign of God, it makes sense that we can make *good* judgments there—to call out sin, call each other forward, spur one another on toward love and good deeds, and so forth. And, on occasion, when it's really necessary, we can cancel a lunch appointment with a brother or sister so that we can, in love, confront a blatant sin. But we cannot and should not impose our truths as disciples upon the external behavior patterns of nondisciples. So when we talk about the authoritative nature of Scripture, it can be applied only inside the family.

Family Caveat

I want to stress here that, while we have some scriptural support for judgment within the church, we have to realize that the law of love should still prevail and guide the depth and level of confrontation. This scripture is not, as some believe, a carte blanche permission slip to be brutal to each other.

From an early age, I recall some terrible examples of poor judgment in the church. In eighth grade, my friend Kristin had to stand onstage at our church and repent in front of the entire congregation for making out with a kid at youth camp. In high school, I remember the pain of having to watch my Led Zeppelin, Aerosmith, and rap CDs burn at the annual New Year "purification" bonfire. Believe me, it wasn't optional if you were to stay in good favor with the rest of the group. In college, just for kicks I tried a Pentecostal church, and a few friends took me aside to make sure I wasn't being drawn into a cult. Postcollege and into adulthood, it seemed like I was in constant judgment from those inside the church over having a beer, hanging out in saloons, being late to the Bible studies, having poor church attendance, and so on. Now that I'm a writer, it gets even uglier. The most personal attacks on my writing always seem to come from inside the ranks with very little attempt to understand my point of view. I wish I could say that I think these events are isolated, but as I've shared a few of my stories, it seems that many people have had similar experiences. By simply watching Christians bash each other on Facebook, it's quite obvious that we still feel our job is to straighten everyone out. In the end, the idea of love covering a multitude of sins takes a backseat to "expose the immoral brother." We're worse than TMZ! I understand the pressure to want to call out false teaching and false teachers, but there is a distinct difference between them. False teachers in the time of the New Testament were people who intentionally tried to lead people astray. Those whom Paul and others felt comfy calling out. But most of the people we call out in no way have a heart to tear the church apart. At worst, they are bad teachers and lousy interpreters of Scripture, history, and context—and God is more than able to weather that storm.

Personally, if I had not grown up in the church, I would have a hard time accepting the truth of Christianity because of all the arguing and disagreements among us. In other words, I wouldn't trust the Bible because the Christians I observed would have no compelling authority in handling the Scriptures.

Pick a New Fight

This statement will probably get me outed, but if the church is to regain respect, we are going to have to stop disassociating with each other and rebuild a sense of family unity, even if our views on certain issues are wide and contentious. We need a new fight.

Let me ask you a question. If you were Jesus and you had just one final prayer for the human race before you left, what would you have asked for? Personally I would have asked for God's help in planting thousands of great churches. Others I've talked to said they would have asked for incredible wealth in which to bless the poor. Others still said Jesus should have asked that one of His disciples become the next reigning king so he could change the political climate. All of these are reasonably strategic requests Jesus could have made, but here is His actual prayer recorded for us in John 17:11:

> I will remain in the world no longer, but they are still in the world, and I am coming to you. Holy Father, protect them by the power of your name, the name you gave me, so that they may be one as we are one.

Just before this prayer, Jesus was actually teaching the disciples and giving them final instructions. In John 13:34–35 He said,

> A new command I give you: Love one another. As I have loved you, so you must love one another. By

this everyone will know that you are my disciples, if
you love one another.

Apparently Jesus leapfrogged over all the things you and I
might have thought more important to spread the gospel of Jesus
throughout the world. But Jesus knew the most important witness
of His new kingdom was His followers being unified in love and
oneness. My guess is Jesus knew that when people would later see us
claiming to be followers but being so divided, so argumentative, so
fervent about things that divide us, our movement wouldn't be very
attractive.

Later on Paul shared critical issues with the church in Ephesus
and reiterated how important this is. Ephesians 4:1–6 reads,

> As a prisoner for the Lord, then, I urge you to live
> a life worthy of the calling you have received. Be
> completely humble and gentle; be patient, bearing
> with one another in love. Make every effort to keep
> the unity of the Spirit through the bond of peace.
> There is one body and one Spirit, just as you were
> called to one hope when you were called; one Lord,
> one faith, one baptism; one God and Father of all,
> who is over all and through all and in all.

Here again we find another major focus of Jesus we often miss.
Jesus knows people will hardly ever agree on anything. That even
people who agree on Scripture's authority may come down on different sides of an issue. I was once reminded that a point of view

is simply a view from a point, and oneness, or unity, can therefore never be based on getting someone to see from your point; instead it is love and unity amid different beliefs. And this is exactly why unity is so powerful. It's almost impossible. And because it is so difficult, Jesus would much prefer we fight for a supernatural form of love and unity instead of fighting against each other or people outside our faith. To put it in plain terms, it's time to stop fighting against sin and sinners, other denominations, liberals, fundies, conservatives, evangelicals, or mainline denominations. It's even time to stop fighting against Catholics, atheists, Rob Bell, Oprah, Driscoll, Piper, nauseating televangelists, or any other Christian leaders you disagree with on certain issues.

I realize that Paul called out a few men for false teaching, but these men were challenging the most central teaching of the gospel regarding Jesus—the cross, or the resurrection. Yeah, these are worth putting your dukes up for, but that's about the only thing we should be fighting about if we are to be unified. Unity can happen only when we shrink down the number of hills we will die on. And according to Paul it's a very small list. For him, it's one Lord, one faith, one baptism, one God who's got all the other stuff under control because He's over all, through all, and in all. Practically, it comes down to this: if someone claims to have put his trust in Jesus for the remission of his sins, based on His death on the cross, he is off-limits! And since we now know we should also not judge those who have not made this decision, it pretty much puts all judgment in the no-go zone! That's what unity is based on.

In Paul's time the church was growing in size through a wide range of ethnicities, customs, worldviews, sin propensities, and traditions; there were thousands of individual stories of people who held varying and divergent beliefs on all matters of faith and life. Paul knew there would be trouble unless he put a more important umbrella of love over all the unloving conclusions they would naturally come to.

Jesus and Paul both knew that our orthopraxy (how we live unto God) would look totally different based on all the divergent cultures and thus gave us permission to have a long leash on what was acceptable and a very short leash on what we should focus on. And if you allow for an accommodating, generous orthopraxy, you have to also allow for some generous, accommodating, permissive orthodoxy.

The unity of the Spirit through the bond of peace means you may not agree with Rob Bell on issues of heaven or hell, and you may think Oprah is the second coming of Beelzebub, but if Rob says he has put his faith in Jesus, then *end of discussion*—at least end of judgmental discussions about where he stands with God. You may have all the discussions you like about his theology, but fighting for unity means you fight the urge to judge on anything other than Jesus, the cross, and someone's faith in Him. And even then you can't judge because you really never know where someone stands or will stand five years in the future. I've found out the hard way that whenever I draw a conclusion about someone's beliefs, I also assume those beliefs are constant. But people change, and since God is always at work in a person's life, I have no right to judge where they will be a month, year, or decade from now. We are all in process, so unity calls for prayer over those we disagree with, not nasty Facebook posts.

This chapter is the most important one for me because it's the most personal. Just this week, two evangelical megachurches came out in full support of LGBT issues. Whereas before they were both loving churches that accepted these people into their membership and allowed communion and service in the church, they also both withheld the marriage ceremony and leadership and staff positions. Now nothing is withheld.

As you can imagine, both pastors have taken a lot of heat. Brimstone-level heat. Many evangelical leaders are calling them heretics and false teachers and, of course, are damning them to hell's fire. In the past, I would have picked up a rock myself, but this time, one of the men is a dear friend, someone who's been in an intimate small group of men with me for the last three years. When the news came out, our group of buddies, all of whom serve in major church and kingdom leadership positions, began to e-mail each other openly about our concerns and our prayers. Within our group we had highly divergent views on the LGBT issues. One e-mail from a conservative, more traditional member began the exchange, and then the pastor of said church responded. I have permission from both men to use their names, but to honor their time and not create any more fights for them, I've decided to change their names. But I do want you to read what they said.

From Joe, the conservative brother who tried to discourage Kevin from changing his church's stance:

Hey, gents, as you know, Kevin and his church have made a big step and come out for full inclusion on the LGBT issue. Marriage. Any position in leadership, etc. A lot of you who know me well know that I don't agree theologically with Kevin on this and that I believe the Bible is clear on this point—in contradiction of what Kevin teaches here. HOWEVER,

I love Kevin. I mean, like really actually. We've talked consistently through this process and I love his heart for the marginalized and outcast in this whole thing. There is no doubt that the LGBT community feels judged by the church and unwelcome there for the most part. And we need to repent of that. It's a big sin and stain on our already well-stained reputation as those bearing the name of Christ. I also know that on this e-mail list we're probably split about 50/50 on this issue. Here's the deal that I want to call out—I've lived with it most of my life. So have many of you. It's this can we REALLY love the sinner while hating his sin? Most of my Muslim friends know that I love them as they are. But all of my close Muslim friends also know that I think they should follow Jesus. And that staying as a typical Muslim caught in the trenches of Islam isn't the best for them. And I'd go on to say, it is actually death for them to stay the way they are (as it is for me to stay the way I am). So sometimes my Muslim friends feel judged by me. They are surprised when they eventually learn I do not believe Muhammad was a Prophet (in the biblical sense as one speaking for God). And for sure not the "final Prophet." They are surprised that I do not believe the Quran has equal authority with the Bible. And they are hurt. They sometimes feel unwelcome by me because of that. On the other hand, many in the Christian world think I've gone WAY too far in "being Muslim to reach Muslims." That I'm too soft on Islam. That I even support the religion of Islam and I'm only hard on Christians. And I think most of you live in this tension. Can we TRULY love the outsider? Completely welcome them in? It's called grace. And yet hold to biblical standards of truth? It's hard frankly. I think we're all trying to do just that. And let's keep holding that tension between Grace and Truth. Jesus was full of both. I want to be too. I don't want to sacrifice one for the other.

In the meantime, let's hold Kevin and the church community and families up in prayer. We don't have to agree on everything to be brothers and friends and colaborers. Let's have their backs when people speak ill of them. Let's defend them to our friends and to our peers. And let's call each other to be better and more Christlike men!

Love you guys,
Joe

Response from Kevin:

Jeez, Joe. I couldn't feel less worthy of this. There have been tons of beautiful/tragic stories and e-mails but also lots of canceled giving statements and angry people. Lots of gossip about all our "issues" from people who never had a problem until we became open and affirming. I've got pastors I've never met confronting me to speak their "truth in love" and churches changing their sermon calendar to now preach against sin and homosexuality. I'm exhausted! But as the intensity mounts, I SO feel like the wrong guy for 1,000 reasons. This wave of criticism and anger feels like an anvil on my back. I'm terrified to fail the LGBTQ community (who have been let down enough) after putting my church and career and everything on the line. Again, not because I'm doubting the decision but because I feel like the 3rd string quarterback taking my first snap in the Super Bowl. So all that whimpering to say I'm humbled by you and thanks for the prayer. Anybody who stands up for fakes and phonies, wimps or JV quarterbacks, especially when they disagree ... Now that's a true friend.

Maybe this is what making every effort to preserve the unity of the Spirit in the bond of peace feels like.

Love you guys,

Kevin

I let you in on a very intimate exchange because I hope you'll get a sense that both sides of very difficult issues happen with people who deeply love Jesus. Both sides of this LGBT argument are from men who have given up their lives to follow Jesus and sacrificially serve the human race. Both men view the Bible as having been inspired by God, use it as their only source of teaching and authority in their church, and both are humbly trying to navigate their missionary contexts with faithful response to Jesus. But serious disagreement exists over this one issue, and instead of separating, defrocking, or dismantling long-standing community and friends, these two men, along with another twenty men in this circle, are challenging each other behind closed doors, praying fervently for one another, begging God for clarity and truth, and fighting for a larger unity. I really believe this is what Jesus encouraged Paul to write about. This fight is a good fight!

I am not comfortable with where Kevin has landed, but I'm also inspired by his love for the marginalized, and it causes me to blow the dust off long-held beliefs with which I've simply not engaged honestly for many years. I feel that as I pray and love my brother who I know is struggling, I, too, must have the courage to look deeper into the issues that Jesus really cares about.

Oh, how this would change the world if we really believed what Jesus believes about people and how to approach them. We must altogether stop making pronouncements; we must stop publishing our stance; we must stop calling out people we don't agree with; and we must, at all cost, say to anyone who puts his faith in Jesus that we are all a part of one big, weird, wacko family of ruffians. And when we do, the world might judge us as finally worthy to hang out with.

In the church—which should be the pillar and support of the truth—you will have brothers and sisters who believe Jonah was actually swallowed by a whale and others who just see it as an allegory or metaphor for a legit spiritual truth. Some will smoke weed and enjoy a nice whiskey, and some will choose to abstain from both. You will have people who are attracted to the same sex (or to both) and those who can't shake their porn addiction for the opposite sex. You will have honest Jesus lovers who think it's showing God's love to go to gay weddings, and even perform them, while others won't feel free to do either. You will have brothers and sisters who believe in a literal hell and think very few will make it to the pearly gates, while others will also take quite a few scriptures literally and believe that Christ's payment for sin is applied far more generously than we can ever imagine. God's church is made up of people who would rise and fall on every word uttered by conservative reformers like John Piper, and His church will have just as many people who love Rob Bell for what he contributes to our struggle as Christians today. The church includes those musty, old Greek and Russian Orthodox priests who make you sit through three-hour church services listening to a language you don't know, and it also includes *Duck Dynasty* fans who agreed with Phil Robertson when

STREET-LEVEL SAINTS   125

he told Fox News's Sean Hannity that in regard to ISIS, "You have to convert them or kill them."

Look, that simply is the church. I know it bugs you as it does me, but consider how darn patient Jesus is, and understand that He wants you to represent Him, not defend Him. He can handle that.

Although some of these issues may seem like deal breakers to you, the Scriptures don't give you the right to make a final call and break off. If you run into someone with views you passionately disagree with, but Jesus and His atoning work on the cross are central to that person's life, then you cannot write him off or boot him out of the family. Remember, it's not your call, but Jesus's, to make. In fact, if you really hope to persuade someone to change his views, fighting for unity and staying friends is your best option.

So I don't argue with people anymore who want to continue to focus on judgment, hell, and the lake of fire. Nor do I challenge or nitpick those who think the lake of fire and the fumes of brimstone are metaphors instead of realities. What I've come to know is that amid all the many flavors, fumes, levels of maturity, depth of knowledge, naivety, and knuckleheads, we all have a sincere desire to tell people about the love of God and the opportunity to live under His reign. In other words, I don't think these varied opinions require that someone burns at the stake, jumps in the lake, smokes a brimstone joint, gets unfriended on Facebook, or is disassociated with. I can call them my brothers and sisters because they believe in the cross of Jesus and are learning as best they can to let Him be the final authority in their lives.

Even if I'm wrong, since Jesus said the highest law of the land is the law of love, I think He'll give me a thumbs-up for doing all

I could to preserve the unity of His body. And having a strong scriptural case that God's grace extends way beyond our simplified ideas of who's saved and who's not allows us to live free of stress and fear. We don't have to scare people out of hell or pressure them into heaven. We have no power in either of these directions anyway. We can instead spend that energy on telling the story of Jesus's inclusive love and subsequent death on the cross so that no one would be stuck under the wrath of his or her own sin. It's a win-win for both sides.

I can enjoy the fellowship of any humble soul who is trying to figure this stuff out as we learn from and challenge each other. For the unhumble, I'm not going to judge them. I'm just not going to give them a second of my day. Life is too short.

All Things to All People

Okay, let's come out of the rabbit hole and get back to the Jesus life we get to live. I think with an open, humble posture toward the Bible, we have far more freedom in how we live on the streets. Listen to how Paul speaks of this more creative way with people in 1 Corinthians 9:19–23:

> Though I am free and belong to no one, I have made myself a slave to everyone, to win as many as possible. To the Jews I became like a Jew, to win the Jews. To those under the law I became like one under the law (though I myself am not under the law), so as to win those under the law. To those not having the law I became like one not having the law

(though I am not free from God's law but am under
Christ's law), so as to win those not having the law.
To the weak I became weak, to win the weak. I have
become all things to all people so that by all possible means I might save some. I do all this for the
sake of the gospel, that I may share in its blessings.

Paul understood that the generosity of God's grace overrode his
normal biases against the diverse people to whom God sent him. To
Jewish people, Paul could act, speak, and be truly Jewish. With the
Roman and Egyptian and Turkish Gentiles, he would tuck Jewish
ways of thinking under his tunic and instead deal with people on
their terms. In one instance, he passionately told the new converts
in Galatia not to let people weigh down their simple faith with a
heavy dose of Jewish constraints. He specifically discouraged them
from getting circumcised. Yet in another town, he made his prodigy
Timothy get circumcised just in case he got caught with his loins
uncovered. It was a good day for the gospel but a lousy day for young
Timothy! The gospel of Jesus never changed in essence, but the wise,
nuanced way it was presented within the different cultures was radi-
cally different.

Just as we learn to have a wider view of God's grace and a more
humble approach to interpreting Scripture, we can naturally loosen
up the edges on what we ask people to consider changing if they want
to be Jesus followers. Instead of imposing requirements on what they
must change, missionary saints ask questions like these:

- What things are essential to bring up now, what can wait until later after we are friends and they trust me, and what needs to wait ten years down the road when they are living intentionally under the rule and reign of Jesus?
- What will be good news to this person, and how do I lead with that?
- What issues should I not make a big deal about?
- What behaviors do I need to overlook?
- What role does timing play in my interactions with this person?
- How must I live in order to get people to respect me and trust my way of life and beliefs?
- What assumptions do they have about Christians, and how can I change their negative assumptions?

It's Gonna Get Hectic; It's Gonna Get Wild!

You might be wondering whether there are any critical essentials left—the have-tos and don't-dos—that we need to teach people as we love them into the kingdom. You wouldn't be the first to wonder this! In Acts 15, we are told the story of Paul, Peter, and some early church leaders who had a big meeting to decide what essential issues of discipleship they should bring up to the hordes of new believers joining their ranks. Remember, all the leaders at this point were Jewish and living according to the Law of Moses and hundreds of other Jewish laws. These were critical to them and had been the right way to live for thousands of years. After a rather tense meeting, they boiled the essentials down to three simple issues: abstain from sexual immorality, from food polluted by idols, and from the meat of strangled animals.

Before we get to those, remember that this was all happening after Jesus had rejoined the Father in heaven. His followers were now trying to live according to the gospel of Christ; they would all have missed God's will had they stuck fast to following the Scriptures and Jewish religious Law to the letter. Indeed, this is what made the meeting so contentious—some were dedicated to living literally according to the Scriptures while others were convinced they could live freely under God's grace as the Spirit directed them.

Paul, Barnabas, and James, who was the leading elder in Jerusalem at the time, were trying to persuade the other leaders to lay aside their long-held patterns of thought and behavior, all "required" by Scripture. How they interpreted the words of Scripture was being altered by real-life issues—their old way of looking at the truth was no longer tenable. God was giving His Spirit to the "outsiders," the non-Jewish people, and the scholars and leaders who knew the Holy Scriptures best had no grid for it. Even Peter struggled with this—he would have made all Gentile believers get circumcised if God hadn't given him a dream to help him see that there was no clean or unclean animal, that circumcision was no longer a requirement to be part of God's people.

Did you catch that? Not only was Scripture taking a backseat to on-the-ground experience, but as Peter related his change of mind to the others, his desire to impose requirements seemed to loosen even more:

> God, who knows the heart, showed that he accepted
> them [the Gentiles] by giving the Holy Spirit to
> them, just as he did to us. He did not discriminate
> between us and them, for he purified their hearts by
> faith. (Acts 15:8–9)

Amazing. If today a large number of Christians stood up for
believers in the gay community by saying, "We know in their hearts
they love Jesus," they would get laughed out of the room. The
argument would quickly be rebutted with, "Who cares about their
hearts? If they really loved Jesus, they would turn from their sinful
ways because the Bible says 'sexual immorality this, wrath of God
that.' So they must not *really* love Jesus."

But check this out. At the end of this important council, James
made this "nonbiblical" announcement:

> It is my judgment, therefore, that we should not
> make it difficult for the Gentiles who are turning
> to God. (v. 19)

James made a judgment on behalf of the council, and it was a
right judgment. He said no one should require Gentiles to be circumcised or to obey other laws of Moses. There were no such entrance
requirements for the family of God anymore. Did he quote Bible
verses to defend his opinion? No, because what the new believers
were experiencing didn't fit their interpretation of Scripture as Jewish
believers and scholars. James had to make a subjective decision based

on a lot of experience, a lot of conversations with people who cared deeply about the church and its mission to the world.

As we talk about this I know there are concerns—and I share them as a Bible guy—but what we've just discussed is also in the Bible, so we cannot minimize what this story means for our story today.

Now, back to the three biggies—abstaining from sexual immorality, from food polluted by idols, and from the meat of strangled animals. Why did they boil down all the Jewish laws to these three? Because these issues kept new Gentile believers from being able to eat with and fellowship with Jewish believers and vice versa. They picked this new set of essentials because they wanted the newly forming church to become a cohesive people. They were fighting for unity!

As Paul said later to the Ephesian church, which was struggling with unity,

> Be completely humble and gentle; be patient, bearing with one another in love. Make every effort to keep the unity of the Spirit through the bond of peace. (4:2–3)

Wow, what would happen if we took *that* literally?

Then Paul gave what I think of as the new three:

> There is one body and one Spirit, just as you were called to one hope when you were called; one Lord, one faith, one baptism; one God and Father of all, who is over all and through all and in all. (Eph. 4:4–6)

Sheesh, it looks again like the three new essentials are just one essential—God is the one final authority and He's got this under control.

In the end, a small band of combatants to the grace-filled gospel of Jesus became known as the Judaizers. They were more concerned about converting people to the Jewish way of faith than the gospel way of faith. It was with the Judaizers that Paul had to fight, and as we seek to missionize this crazy culture around us, we would be wise not to become the Christianizers or Evangelicalizers.

Back to the Mission Next Door

So let's go on a mission together with Jesus. Welcome to 2020, a world in which marijuana, gambling, the lottery, and same-sex marriage is legal in every state. Polygamy is up for a vote again, and interest groups are pushing hard to legalize all forms of drugs. Undocumented immigrants from every country have been grandfathered in and allowed immediate citizenship, bringing their religious, cultural, and political intricacies with them. America remains a free nation, and people who follow Islam are running for office, intent on legalizing a call to prayer at four o'clock in the morning over loudspeakers in every city with a mosque.

Look, the church of the future will look almost exactly like the *Star Wars* bar scene—almost no one will look "normal." So get used to it, strap on a sense of humor, loosen up your religion and your stuffy attitude, and get your missionary mojo fired up. These are your new neighbors, the ones Jesus is calling you to be on mission for, the ones you must learn how to love as much as you love your own life. These are the blessed ones He refers to when He says, "I have other sheep that are not of this sheep pen. I must bring them also" (John 10:16). It's going to get crazy, but you don't need to fear it. To help keep your wits about you, just remember the hinge point: love God with all you've got, and love your neighbor just as much.

What do we know for sure?

- The Bible is a believer's main source of information about God, self, others, and life together.
- The authority of the Bible is not in our interpretation of it but in the real God behind it.
- In our poor handling of the Word of truth, we have become bad missionaries using the words of Scripture to judge against instead of to draw to.
- God expects us to think and act like a missionary, getting past literalism and trusting the Spirit to guide us to the heart of the matter.

What should we change in light of what we know?

- We should hold our interpretations lightly and be more humble with people who see truth from another angle.
- We should not make it hard for people to come to faith by imposing our essentials on them.

- We should not be people of the letter of the law but of the heart of the letter.
- We must now consider that God's church will be made up of people who interpret the Bible differently, so we must be gracious and patient, listen, and do all we can to keep the doors open.

Who might this change affect, and what is God asking you to do?

- Who have you written off, kicked out, or kept out?
- Consider attending another religious gathering just to see how others practice their faith in God.
- Consider buying a new translation of the Bible. Whenever and whatever you read, stop and ask this question: "What is God's heart behind these words?"

Why is this good news for you?

- The Bible can now be a guide for how you live, not just what you believe.
- You may be coming into a new season where God will lead you as a missionary saint. Get ready to see some cool things happen with people.

7

OUR CLANDESTINE CALLING: RETHINKING RECONCILIATION

You can tell you've created God in your own image
when He hates the same people you do.

—Tom Weston

The dream finally happened—we are empty nesters. After twenty-three years of marriage, twenty of which were centered around our son Ryan's severe epilepsy, we finally unloaded all our kids and got Cheryl the horse ranch she's always wanted. Nothing fancy, just four acres with a cool barn and three horse stalls. Personally, I'm not a horse guy, but I figured I needed to learn so I could ride with her. When we moved in, we rented a room to an actual cowboy named Grahm.

One day I asked Grahm to help me learn how to ride. We saddled the steeds and headed out to the round pen just below our property. The round pen seemed like a good idea at the time because I figured if anything went wrong, I could just jump the rails and escape. Grahm started me off pretty slow. He sat atop Cheryl's horse, Layla, and I was mounted securely on DJ. Grahm led me in a game of follow the leader. I just kept my horse in first gear and walked slowly in figure-eight patterns inside the circle.

For some equine reason, these horses don't really like each other, but it never occurred to Grahm or me that anything would go wrong inside the pen … until it did. I parked my horse at the fence, and Grahm parallel parked his rig right next to mine. We enjoyed a five-minute cowboy-to-cowboy chat, and then I decided I wanted to do a little more work. I gave my twelve-hundred-pound pet a little pressure with my heels. She took one step forward and then began to kick Layla. Layla wheeled around and attacked back. For the next minute or so, the horses went round and round, hooves flying, dust clouds billowing, and the sound of smacks filling the air almost as if the hooves were striking flesh rather than hide. Oh, they were, and the flesh was mine. I took three solid blows and the last one really hurt, so I took a risk and spurred my ride hard, hoping she would take the cue and get the heck away from Layla. But she didn't like that and sent me flying! Yep, first ride in twenty years and two-thirds of my body was black and blue; my pride looked even uglier. The worst part was that Cheryl had watched the whole thing from our deck. She came down and said, "Nice first ride, cowboy."

That day I learned a lot of things, the most poignant lesson being that trying to reconcile two angry beasts is hard to do.

In 2 Corinthians 5:11, 14–20, we get a really clear picture of our main job description while we're on earth:

> Since, then, we know what it is to fear the Lord, we try to persuade others…. For Christ's love compels us, because we are convinced that one died for all, and therefore all died. And he died for all, that those who live should no longer live for themselves but for him who died for them and was raised again. So from now on we regard no one from a worldly point of view. Though we once regarded Christ in this way, we do so no longer. Therefore, if anyone is in Christ, the new creation has come: The old has gone, the new is here! All this is from God, who reconciled us to himself through Christ and gave us the ministry of reconciliation: that God was reconciling the world to himself in Christ, not counting people's sins against them. And he has committed to us the message of reconciliation. We are therefore Christ's ambassadors, as though God were making his appeal through us.

As I've said, *Brimstone* is about God's mission becoming our mission. But this passage takes this highfalutin idea and brings it down to a very clear job description, and it's a privilege for all Jesus followers. We have been given the same business card Jesus had—we are to be reconcilers. I guess it sounds more spiritual to call it a ministry of reconciliation, but as you'll see, it's really a secret, mysterious dance of bringing far-out and far-off people together toward the center that is Jesus.

Just tonight on the news, there are three main stories. The first covers the riots in Ferguson, Missouri, occurring because a white police officer shot a young, unarmed black man. The second story is about Iraqi Christians who are being slaughtered by militant Muslims, and the last is about the fighting between Israeli and Palestinian forces in the never-peaceful West Bank. When I see these, I can't help but think as many do—there's just no way to bring these two twelve-hundred-pound beasts together. Dust is flying, hooves are flailing, and apart from a true miracle, it almost seems impossible to find peace, doesn't it? But whether it is massive global tensions, the everyday chasm between evangelicals and the gay community, or the street-level gap between the church and the unchurched, our call is to do what we can to bring people closer to the center, and the center is Jesus.

So let's get into this study of reconciliation and find some practical pointers to help us do a better job.

The Art of Persuasion

People who know me call me an evangelist. I've always been uncomfortable with that because it conjures up images of an overbearing TV personality who tries to scam money off naive viewers, or of a loud, ADD street preacher screaming Bible verses at uninterested and annoyed pedestrians. So most of the time I try to distance myself from the word.

But that Corinthians passage has given me a label that actually warms my heart, and I think it's a better description of what evangelism actually is.

I am a persuader. And evangelism is the spirit-led art of getting people closer to Jesus so they can be persuaded.

Persuasion simply means the act of causing people to believe something they wouldn't naturally. But persuasion done right is not so much trying to get people to see what we see as much as it is trying to get people to see what God sees.

With each seeing only their own side, the only way to bring about reconciliation is by inserting something new into the conflict that neither side is focusing on. Something that will help everyone involved see the situation differently or find something more important or bigger than what is right in front of their faces.

For Jesus, for Paul, and hopefully for us, the concept that helps us introduce the bigger picture is the good news. You see, if the gospel is only about doctrine, then we have to get people to listen to it, and then we have to argue over points of perceived truth about it and whether or not our interpretations are accurate. But the good news transcends all of that nonsense. Sharing the gospel is simply persuading people with a win versus a loss. Maybe if we could rise above doctrinal conflict together and show peaceful humility, conversation, and even friendship, we could see mountains moved.

Since the gospel is always about good news, in our struggle to be reconcilers we always ask ourselves,

"Is this conversation moving in a good direction?"
"Are good feelings growing between this person
    and me?"
"Is what I'm doing with this person a good use of
    my time?"

"Does this person have a good reason to continue
  the dialogue with me?"
"Would this person share good things about me
  with his or her friends?"
"Am I helping this person see the goodness of God
  in how I am interacting with him or her?"

Persuasion is not about a moment-in-time conversion. Persuasion is a process by which we continually offer *good* reasons to keep talking, keep moving, keep going toward the center, which is Jesus.

Jesus in the Center

Are you starting to see why Jesus is so important in bringing people together? Many of us really do have a heart to see people come to Jesus, but this right motive often takes a wrong turn when we try to coerce or persuade through guilt or judgments about beliefs and behaviors.

This is why Jesus said in John 14:9, "Anyone who has seen me has seen the Father." It's easy to overlook the simplicity of this. Jesus was simply saying, "Don't put anything else in front of people other than Me. Don't talk about church, don't talk about Bible verses, don't talk about their sins, don't talk about the religion of Christianity, don't talk about bad Christians or bad Muslims or what was on the news. None of these draw people to God. Try to keep people focused on Me."

For some miraculous reason, Jesus seems to transcend all the bogus stuff that religion and humans do. That's why we must always stick Him in the middle of the room, in the middle of the conversation, or remind people about Him. He works.

"But, Hugh, I just can't stand Christians." I'm not asking you to be a Christian or like them. I'm asking you to consider following Jesus.

"Hugh, throughout history Christians have done terrible things to people who didn't believe what they believed." Yep, I know, but Jesus didn't do any of those things, nor did He want those things to happen.

"Hugh, it seems like religion does so much harm and very little good in the world." I agree and so does Jesus. That's why He came to put an end to religion.

"Hugh, I don't believe the Bible is trustworthy, so how can I figure out who God is?" Actually Jesus's life and teachings are pretty well documented by reliable scholars. And Jesus did say that if you look at Him, you'll know exactly what God is like. Could you consider just reading the stories about Him or His words?

"Hugh, God seems so mean in the Old Testament. I just don't get it." Yes, He does, but the best way to really see God is to look at Jesus. Jesus said, "Anyone who has seen me has seen the Father."

I've had a thousand conversations like these if I've had one, and I can tell you that Jesus doesn't offend people. He often changes their assumptions, but at the very least He is able to keep the conversation moving forward in a positive fashion. Arguing about beliefs, quoting Bible verses, and belittling people for their behavior almost always leaves people estranged, but Jesus is a salve to religious wounds, a calming presence when emotions are ready to erupt, and a voice of reason amid swirling opinions. Keep Him in the center.

Beer Goggles

Maybe you've heard jokes about how being under the influence of alcohol can warp your sensibilities and perceptions. "Beer goggles" means you've had one too many, and now you see a man or woman in a positive light rather than recognizing the person for the human he or she really is. Well, here's the next secret of reconciliation. You have to see people differently—you have to put on different lenses.

Have you ever seen *Undercover Boss*? It's a cool show in which the rich owners of companies dress down and act like rookie employees in their own companies to see what is actually happening. In an episode that had me blubbering, the CEO ends up deeply touched by four employees. He reveals his true identity at the end of the show and then blesses each person with raises, relocations, and better positions. Since he had been with them, his perspective of how he treated his employees changed.

We've already talked about this a little, but remember to always try to see people through Genesis 1, not Genesis 3, eyes. See them as creations of God with the image of God as their face. If you focus on sin, behavior, attitudes, and beliefs, it will be hard to want to draw them to the center. But if you see every human as someone under redemptive reconstruction, you'll find great motivation to work with Jesus instead of making His job harder.

It's easy to see how reconciliation and persuasion become more difficult when we count people's sins against them rather than focusing on the image of God in them. If someone tried to restore a friendship with me by shoving my face in my sin, I'd tell him to buzz off. But that's not Jesus's way.

What? Don't people need to feel guilt over their sins before they can turn to God? Evidently not. Or at least not as the first step. It appears that judgment over sins runs counter to the reconciliation process. Jesus knows from firsthand experience that finger pointing never creates an atmosphere of openness. This is why Paul, in teaching us about the law of love, says love covers over a multitude of sins. So put on your God goggles and stop bringing up sins. Stop doing it with your own children, stop arguing over political points at the office, and by all means, put on your God goggles and start looking for signs of life, signs of humanity, and the image of God that's there rather than signs of death.

Direction Instead of Perfection

Jesus never focused on where a person was spiritually but where that person was going spiritually. I've heard a lot of different renderings of the process most people go through as they grow, but one that is quite interesting was explained in a book called *Move*, published by Zondervan in 2011. After Willow Creek Association surveyed one thousand churches, they found there were four distinct categories of growth for most people.

- **Exploring Christ:** These people are searching for God and are what we might call "checking Jesus out."
- **Growing in Christ:** These people are those who are open to God, have a basic belief, and are trying to learn things about God.

- **Close to Christ:** These people are on personal terms with God and are actively trying to adjust certain parts of their lives to the teaching of Jesus.
- **Christ Centered:** These people are totally surrendered to God and view every decision through the lens of true obedience, regardless of cost.

It won't surprise you to find out that very few American Christians fit the final category, the category many of us would call "sold out" or "good Christians." Stats show, in fact, that most Christians in America fall between stages two and three. Interestingly, Jesus speaks of wanting to spit from His mouth the lukewarm because they are neither hot nor cold. Many would hear this in light of these findings and think, *Well, then, most of those people are in big trouble*—and if we are literalists, then many may not make it to heaven at all. A more reasonable understanding of the larger biblical story pushes us instead to see people with good hearts who are working toward growth in each and every step. This is what Jesus sees. I think the tone of this warning from God is more about direction than perfection. Lukewarm refers to someone who intentionally stops growing and stays in a state of stunted growth and maturity.

This is important because relinquishing your judgment requires that you see people in the context of process—even their sin and sinful patterns of behavior. Your goal should not be to completely, instantaneously change the other person but rather to encourage simple movement forward. The direction a person or contentious issue is heading must become more important than perfecting the person or situation. I'm not sure if you've noticed, but there were a lot of social ills that existed in the times of Abraham, Moses, the prophets, and Jesus. There was slavery, sexism, oppressive work environments, religious legalism, and over-the-top "justice" as bad as modern-day Islamic Sharia law. You'd get stoned for just about anything! There was sexual promiscuity, divorce, alcoholism, and oppressive racism. Based on the right standards of God, you'd think Jesus would have shown up and started going down the checklist of all the social ills of society, calling them out one by one and mobilizing people to go after the offenders. But Jesus knew better. He knew that to go after specific issues would be a trap. One such instance is found in Matthew 22:15–22.

> Then the Pharisees went out and laid plans to trap him in his words. They sent their disciples to him along with the Herodians. "Teacher," they said, "we know that you are a man of integrity and that you teach the way of God in accordance with the truth. You aren't swayed by others, because you pay no attention to who they are. Tell us then, what is your opinion? Is it right to pay the imperial tax to Caesar or not?" But Jesus, knowing their evil intent, said, "You hypocrites, why are you trying to trap me? Show me the coin used for paying the tax." They brought him a denarius, and he asked them, "Whose image is this? And whose inscription?"

"Caesar's," they replied. Then he said to them, "So give back to Caesar what is Caesar's, and to God what is God's." When they heard this, they were amazed. So they left him and went away.

To pay taxes to Caesar wasn't a clean scenario. People knew that Caesar, considered a Roman god himself, was against the God of the Jews. They also knew there was incredible corruption around the taxes they paid and that their tax rates were way beyond fair. So why didn't Jesus say that? Why didn't He call out Caesar and say, "I wouldn't pay the scumbag. He's ripping everyone off, he's selfish and greedy, and you're probably only paying him because you're afraid to rise up and confront him."

Jesus didn't say any of this because He was smart. He knew that to take too big a jump too fast would only create more trouble, the type of trouble that makes it really hard for reconciliation to occur. So He said something that would actually bridge the space a little. Jesus didn't call out the role of women in society, He didn't politicize racism, sexism, sexual orientation, or slavery. But He did close the distance on every one of these issues. He spoke to women respectfully and lovingly, so women were eventually allowed to be in home church gatherings forty years later. He cared for non-Jewish people, and thus as the churches formed and expanded, a church converged in Antioch where different ethnicities, different skin colors, and different societal points of view flourished.

This again is why you want to keep Jesus in the conversation. Jesus and His teachings may not have fixed all the social ills in an instant, but everything He said and did absolutely moved the issues forward. If we keep this in mind when working through the process of reconciliation, it will help keep our posture humble and our perspective positive.

Gotta Get Personal

The other day I was watching a story on Golf Channel about a man who had chosen to become anatomically altered into a woman. He had a lovely wife and golfed weekly with his three buddies. In many respects he had a perfectly normal life. But underneath it all was a lifelong struggle of feeling like his body did not reflect his gender. After the operation, she and her wife divorced but remained strong friends. And, of course, she finally told her golfing mates.

One of the men was what you might call a classic Rush Limbaugh–type fellow. When asked how he felt when she confronted him with her new identity, he teared up and told the story of how she used to drive long distances to help his family through a really rough time. He then said, "Judgment begins to fade when you relate personally with a … person. When you know their true traits, when you see the other side, the good sides, and when you have a deep emotion of love." And then he ended with, "And this person is my friend."

Nothing will help you relax judgments and be a reconciler better than becoming a friend. We've talked about this a lot already, but I bring it up again because after training hundreds of thousands of pastors and even more normal folks, as obvious as it seems, I've discovered that most of us just don't get across the street.

We may have a few couples over once, or bake some cookies for a neighbor once, or wave at the guy across the street on occasion, but

darn it if we don't take seriously the power of friendship in the reconciliation process. Many have said, "Hugh, I get it, but I really am
not good at making new friends. I'm super busy and I'm an introvert.
So is there a key to this friend thing?" I always respond with just one
answer: "Eat with someone."

Jesus was called a friend of sinners because He ate with them. Pure
and simple. All this means is He conversed and asked questions, and
somehow, over hummus and pita and bad red wine, Jesus could smile
across the table at a tax-collecting swindler. He could sit there and look
past the weird spiritual worship theology of the Samaritan woman, or
roll His eyes and wink at Peter, who constantly did dumb stuff. My
guess is that even when one of His best young friends, Judas, betrayed
Him, He felt compassion for him because of the confusion and pain
He saw in Judas's face as they reclined at their last meal together.

Friends have that funny way with each other. We all have friends
with unique, weird, and annoying personality traits, idiosyncrasies,
and patterns of behavior that we learn to overlook. Why? Because
they are our friends and we love them.

Herein lies a truism about getting over judgment: you can't
judge what you love, and really it's much easier to love someone you
eat with.

So without adding anything to your schedule, you can be part of
the reconciliation process simply by eating one, two, or a few of the
twenty-one meals you have to eat each week with some other people.
I know you're only one person, but consider what would happen if
all ten people in your small group gave up one meal a week. In just
one year you will have given away 560 hours of friendship, and this
can change the world.

Smashing Boxes and Limiting Lines

In 2013, World Vision, the prolific and well-respected Christian relief agency, changed its stance on gay marriage within the organization. World Vision's hiring policy, like most Christian organizations, focused on finding fellow believers who fit within orthodox lines and boxes to be employees. I'm sure there were exceptions and blurred lines, but couples who chose to work there had to be heterosexual in orientation. But in 2013 they decided to open up their hiring policies to include same-sex couples. Within seconds of the decision being made public, people went berserk! Some were ecstatic and some were irate. Although support came from both within and outside the Christian community, all the opposition came from within the ranks. High-profile pastors from around the world publically condemned the change of policy, money was pulled, sponsored kids went without their normal food and clothing rations. And in the end, the pressure outweighed whatever benefits there may have been. Many people expressed outrage that Christian moral codes took precedent over the main thrust of World Vision's mission—caring for the poorest of the poor. Even so, within just a few days, World Vision recanted its decision and returned to the original hiring policy.

Of course, there are hundreds of similar stories and thousands of organizations that hire according to specific Christian values. And, yes, for many there are good reasons to stay true to these decisions. But I have to admit this one had me scratching my head. I remember thinking, *Okay, Halter, if you were in charge and your goal was to feed and care for the practical needs of as many kids around the world as you could, and if you also wanted to use your organization's values and ministry to share the love of God with the world, to publically proclaim the gospel message of Christ's payment for the sins of the whole world and to influence people toward Christ by letting them see what you do, and if you were going to do it alongside your gospel-oriented staff, then you would carefully screen your applicants to make sure no wackos got in. But you'd probably also blow open the doctrinal boxes and limit the lines drawn to keep people from working with you.*

Seriously, what could be a better environment for reconciliation than having all sorts of unlike people participating in what God cares about?

And as the world watched the drama play out, the only thing people outside the faith could conclude was that it had nothing to do with God. The decision once again showed that Christians stay within their own circles, hold their personal values or morality over people, and are willing to partner only with people who believe what they believe and have sex the way they do.

The financial supporters and good-hearted believers who "won" may have perceived the reinstatement of the old policy to be a last-minute three-point shot of victory over darkness.

But maybe it was just another basket for the opposition.

The Kingdom Is Not Ours

After Jesus declared that the kingdom of God was at hand, He publically displayed it and invited people to dip their toes in. The disciples were not the superstar Christians we typically think they were. They were clueless blokes, as were all the other followers Jesus had. Jesus had no moral code that forbade people from helping Him do His kingdom work, nor did He make them reach a certain level of knowledge or behavioral modification before He called them to Himself. My guess is Jesus knew the better play was to get as many people as close to the center as He could so reconciliation could happen as easily as possible.

I realize there are all sorts of problematic issues, but it is worth raising the tension on this so we might make better decisions. If we hold our Christian standards and moral codes as the highest goals of our organizations, then our standards will become what is known about us and said about us. But if we want Jesus to be the thing talked about, maybe our boxes and lines do more harm than good.

Let me ask in the simplest way I can: How can you influence people when you don't allow them to be with you? We don't get to keep people out of the kingdom of God, but we do get to draw people in. We cannot demonstrate the gospel while at the same time demonstrating against a person's sin or lifestyle choices.

So let's consider stepping out of some boxes and removing some lines in the sand, and maybe removing the slogans and propaganda that have publically held the gospel of Jesus hostage. If we are to create a neutral space for the good news of God's kingdom to become tangible, even the names of "our" businesses speak too loudly.

Why oh why do we name our businesses after Jesus? Just the "community" coffee shops alone make me squirm—Higher Grounds Coffee Shop, Holy Grounds, Jehovah Java, He-Brew … These may seem catchy and you might think that goofy slogans will cause a spiritually hungry person to pull over and kneel before the altar of Jesus juice, but it isn't helpful. To be honest, Jesus probably thinks your coffee sucks and is on His way right now to Starbucks, where normal people go. Seriously! If I wanted my coffee shop to draw and influence unbelievers, I'd probably name it something like Hugh's Coffee Joint so that normal people who need a job might come work for me instead of assuming we hire only our own.

A year or so back, Jon Foreman, the lead singer of the popular band Switchfoot, was put on the spot when he was asked if they were a Christian band. Jon said,

> To be honest, this question grieves me because I feel that it represents a much bigger issue than simply a couple SF tunes. In true Socratic form, let me ask you a few questions: Does Lewis or Tolkien mention Christ in any of their fictional series? Are Bach's sonatas Christian? What is more Christ-like, feeding the poor, making furniture, cleaning bathrooms, or painting a sunset? There is a schism between the sacred and the secular in all of our modern minds. The view that a pastor is more "Christian" than a girls volleyball coach is flawed and heretical. The stance that a worship leader is more spiritual than a janitor is condescending and flawed....
>
> None of these songs has been born again, and to that end there is no such thing as Christian music. No. Christ didn't come and die for my songs, he came for me. Yes. My songs are a part of my life. But judging from scripture I can only conclude that our God is much more interested

in how I treat the poor and the broken and the
hungry than the personal pronouns I use when
I sing. I am a believer. Many of these songs talk
about this belief. An obligation to say this or do
that does not sound like the glorious freedom
that Christ died to afford me. I do have an obligation, however, a debt that cannot be settled by
my lyrical decisions. My life will be judged by my
obedience, not my ability to confine my lyrics to
this box or that.[1]

Attaboy, Jon! Like Foreman, we want God to come out of the
closet and be seen for who He is, and we want the world to see
His power. But it doesn't happen when we're afraid of culture or
proud about our morals. We must instead look for every opportunity
to place our way of life, based on our faith, smack-dab next to the
world's disbelief without judging or requiring them to live like us.
There's nothing to fear. God's got this.

Coons in Chicken Feathers

I guess the only thing left to bring up regarding our incredible
opportunity to be reconcilers is that we need to watch out for the
flock, the ones God warns about. In John 10:16, Jesus was speaking
to people who were trying to be bouncers for their religion. He
made them all go cross-eyed when He said, "I have other sheep
that are not of this sheep pen. I must bring them also. They too will
listen to my voice, and there shall be one flock and one shepherd."

Jesus was talking about all of us, and He was standing up to the religious moral police, the coons dressed in chicken feathers, so that someday the gospel would be able to get into our ears and our hands. He took one for us.

We are living in a unique moment in the history of the church, and I think Jesus is asking us to start confronting the gatekeepers head-on as He did. Jesus is building a church for the world, and He needs you and me to stop fearing the fundies and fight for the freaks. Just as Jesus removed the accusers around the woman caught in adultery, we need to stand up in our small groups, march into elder meetings, buy a cup of coffee for our pastors and those who care the most about God's church, and start asking some hard questions. Don't do it to be a jerk and don't judge them either, but for holy heaven, let's talk as brothers and sisters about the real issues. It may be a threat to your church, but it's not a threat to Jesus's church.

As we close on what I hope you find to be the central chapter of this book, go online and check out this story that Penn Jillette (an outspoken atheist and half of the comedy duo Penn and Teller) tells.[2] He shares about the time a gentleman approached him after a show and gave him a Gideons Bible. You would think this would not have been received well, but this time it worked. Why? Simply put, the man acted like a normal guy and related to Penn like he was a human rather than a sinner doomed to hell, and it made all the difference in the world.

Look, I'm not trying to get you to just be neutral in the world. I want you to be able to share your faith, and I want you to wear Jesus on your sleeve. The kingdom is shown, but it is also proclaimed— and the two go hand in hand when people look each other in the eye, drop the religious BS, and are simply kind to one another. The gospel is generous and subversive, not offensive and obtrusive.

What do we know for sure?

- The most privileged part of our calling in Christ is to be reconcilers of the world.
- Persuasion happens best when everything is kept as "good news."
- People will be repelled by almost everything religious except for Jesus, so keep Him in the center.

What should we change in light of what we know?

- We cannot view people from a worldly point of view. Always see a person as someone God is right now trying to woo to Himself. Ask the question, "Am I helping God or making His job harder? Am I helping move this person toward Jesus or repelling him or her?"

Who might this change affect, and what is God asking you to do?

- Are there any people you might need to apologize to for being overbearing, not listening well, giving up on them, or outright judging them?

Consider meeting in person or at least writing an e-mail to them.

- In my family, my ministry, or my work, have I created any boxes or lines that keep people from coming toward Jesus? How can I remove them?

Why is this good news for you?

- I'm not responsible to close the deal, fix, or save anyone. That means I can always view my own faithfulness to Jesus by how well I am drawing people toward the good news of God's kingdom. And I get to live it myself!

8

WHAT ABOUT ALL THE BUTTS, I MEAN BUTS?

God is great, beer is good, and people are crazy.
—Billy Currington

Just this week I was walking through Times Square with a buddy. If you haven't been there, it's interesting: amid all the people, lights, and city noises you'll see little Jesus vendors about every hundred yards or so. Some quietly pass out tracts, some hold up big signs, and some just stand there and preach. No matter what their style, all of their messages focus on hell, sin, sinners, and dying. Not one mentions love, the kingdom of God, heaven, abundant life, or anything related to living now (you know, the stuff Jesus talked about all the time). As you can imagine, not only are they not attracting a crowd, but every person I hear conversing with them is heated, upset, argumentative, and clearly not drawn to their bad news disguised as good news.

Now that the end is near (of the book), I hope you're beginning to see how you can live a beautiful, Jesus-centered life without
judgment. But if you're like me, I know there are still a lot of butts.
No, not the people holding the signs. I meant buts—you know, real,
honest questions about a world with less judgment.

Case in point, I was speaking at a large church one day about
loving your crazy neighbors, and a very shy woman approached me
in tears after the service. She said her heart was exploding with desire
to do this, and she knew theologically that Jesus wanted her to love
her neighbors, but she just had one small problem. Apparently ten
years earlier, a man broke into her home, killed her husband, and
almost killed her. Now her newest neighbor was a pot-smoking,
music-blasting man who had threatened violent retribution if she
ever called the police on him. This dear lady had been in counseling
since losing her husband, was constantly fighting panic attacks, and
clearly loved Jesus. As she recounted these horrific events, she began
to sob again and said, "I want to love this neighbor, but I feel so
guilty because I can't. What should I do with him?"

Living in this world and trying to please Jesus really does have
some sticky spots. Let's remember that the ministry of reconciliation
is about doing all you can to provide a space where people can be
drawn to Jesus or doing all you can to keep unity among the saints.
But it's no guarantee that it always works well or easy, or at all. As
Romans 12:18 says, "If it is possible, as far as it depends on you,
live at peace with everyone." Thank goodness they put that word *if*
in there. The reality is that reconciliation doesn't always work, and
many times it will fail because people are sinful, psycho, immature, or
maybe even on drugs. You are not to judge them, but it doesn't mean

you can't protect yourself from dangerous situations and people, or that sometimes you won't simply have to settle for "I tried my best." Being a nonjudger also means you can't judge yourself, and this woman doesn't need to feel bad that she still has panic attacks and long-term posttraumatic stress symptoms. She is allowed to take care of herself and pick another neighbor to try to love. Nonjudgment doesn't mean nonsense.

Okay, now let's try to look at some other "buts."

Here's a good one: *But if we don't judge people, won't we just get walked over? Won't the world continue to get worse and worse?*

No, the world is getting worse and worse all on its own, and judgment seems to be part of the problem. On any given week the world news bears witness to this, and this week alone confirms that judgment is deeply problematic. On the global front, we have just had an American journalist beheaded by an Islamic faction that judges all religions outside of their tribal sect of Islam as worthy of death. In Ferguson, Missouri, we have potentially explosive racial tension over the shooting of a young black man by a white policeman. It didn't help that one of the police veterans went on a publicized rant about his right and willingness to shoot anyone who steps in front of him … just after touting his faith in the Lord Jesus Christ and his firm belief in the Bible. Outside of natural disasters, which almost everyone but Pat Robertson believes happen without respect or bias, most wars, famine, pestilence, tension, and violence seem to hover around people's biases against other people because of their religious beliefs.

I had an atheist friend dare me to try to convert him to my religion. I said, "Actually, with all the judgment and divisiveness I see around religion, I don't blame you at all for wanting to steer a hundred miles clear of all this mess."

Confused, he replied, "That's the best you got?"

I said, "Yeah, as far as religion goes. I have no interest in converting you to that. But I would love for you to consider taking a serious look at the teaching and life of Jesus because you won't find any of that junk connected to Him. In fact, you'll find He was more ticked off about it than you." With that we started meeting every Tuesday and quite soon he began to follow Jesus.

Let's dive deeper into normal human interactions that I'm sure will happen to you along the way.

Annoyances

First, let's skip over all the standard drive-by annoyances that test your patience with people. These are the people who cut you off in traffic or stay in the left passing lane when they aren't passing. The parents on planes who seem hell-bent on not asking their five-year-old to stop kicking the seat in front of them (which happens to be your seat). The people who go through the fifteen-items-or-less checkout with forty-nine items. (Oh, wait, I do that.) The customer service representative for almost anything you call about who happens to *not* have an easy-to-understand English accent, thus making it almost impossible to understand what he says. And, of course, the airplane or elevator farters. I'm convinced these people are put on the earth to test our moxie.

In each of these cases, though, there is a choice: I can let every idiot I have the misfortune of coming across steal the joy from my day, or I can learn to force a smile before my natural, fleshly urge to kill them takes over. Simply inhaling and exhaling before blowing up is always what the Spirit of God desires—except in the case of the airplane farter. Don't inhale on that one! Seriously, to become a nonjudger, you have to start with mental training wheels to change yourself from the inside out and learn to laugh at the human race instead of wishing it would change.

Family and Friends

If you haven't noticed, we tend to be most judgmental with people closest to us. The reason is that we get hurt most by the people we love. This is why marriage is such a double-edged sword—it is the most intimate of human relationships, so it feels awesome when couples treat each other well, but it hurts more than any other relationship when they don't. The same goes for estrangement between fathers and sons, mothers and daughters, and brothers and sisters, let alone the in-laws.

I know this personally because when Cheryl and I got married as young, fervent Christians, we spent the first three years beating the figurative devil out of each other. We got in fights every day, and every fight seemed like the world was coming to an end, all because we were holding each other to the values of Christian perfection. Our marriage, by the way, changed in an instant when we both realized God did not give us the Bible to use as a weapon but as a guide on how to let love cover a multitude of sins. We haven't had a big fight now for eighteen years! We try to root for each other and be each other's fan instead of booing one another for botched plays.

As a pastor, I've watched and counseled hundreds of people who let momentary mistakes linger for years. Dads who stop talking to daughters, the brother who hasn't called his sister for twelve years because she wrecked his car in high school, the son-in-law who can't stand his mother-in-law and now the tension is destroying his own marriage, and on it goes.

Judgment over family members or past friends weakens when you remember a few things and a question to ask for each of them.

One: Everyone has a bad day. Do you want people judging you based on your worst moments? And if not, how can you help others have a better day?

Two: God is always at work in a person's life. Are you being a part of His redemptive plan or making His job harder? Which side are you on right now?

Three: Feelings of guilt are good because they can create true remorse, but shame is destructive and causes people to be too afraid to come clean. What are you doing to remove another person's shame so it's easier for him or her to say, "I'm sorry for that"? How can you take the lead in the apology?

Four: Verbally calling out the plank in your eye is the best way to help a friend or family member see the speck in his or her eye. What do you need to say sorry for? What mistake or character flaw of your own can you bring up to this person before you express your feelings about his or her situation or behavior?

Five: One in three people in the world is struggling with a mental illness. My own sister has had a fifty-three-year battle with schizophrenia, so I know this for sure. No matter how well you act or how perfect all the conditions may be around this person, the mentally ill *do not* have the capacity to change or act better. So whether you know someone has a mental illness or not, consider that you may be the only person to overlook his weird ways and make his day a little less traumatic.

Six: Every dad or mom has a first name. What I mean by this is that when you've been hurt by a parent, maybe even terribly abused physically, sexually, or emotionally, it's almost a sure bet your mom or dad was hurt the same way by his or her parents. The best advice I can give you is to come to a point where you can call your parent by his or her name rather than Dad or Mom. Sometimes seeing them outside their roles as parents will help you remove your judgment that they dropped the ball along the way, because maybe they never had anyone to help them mature, heal, or repent.

Social Issues

I started this book talking about a gay issue because I feel that if we can learn how to graciously navigate through the many dilemmas related to it, then we can also get through the other social tensions easier. So let's look at some of these big "buts."

But if we don't fight the gay agenda politically, won't the sanctity of marriage be torn down? Nope. Remember, the sanctity of marriage is anchored in God. He thought it up, and no matter how poorly we live out our marriages or how we may redefine it, a marriage between a man and a woman—and your marriage—will always be sacred. If gay marriage becomes legal, yes, some of your tax dollars will help that cause, but a good chunk of your money already goes to stuff you don't believe in. You have a right to vote your conscience, so for sure vote as you believe you should. But once the law is set, the money will be spent, and you're going to have to learn to live with the tension of some political losses.

But then the homosexual agenda will be taught in schools! Yes, it probably will, just like evolution and how to put on a condom. But making disciples has never been up to the secular world. We are to pass on the faith as moms and dads, brothers, sisters, and friends. No matter what is taught on the chalkboard (or iPads), the way you live and what you teach your children is always more powerful. That is, if you take your God-given role seriously and start talking more openly about sex and social issues. We win very few social battles from a political angle. But we can win a ton of personal battles if we take the challenge.

But what if my neighbors are gay? Take heart … at least their lawn will be well kept (joke). Well, here's your chance to initiate a new stage of growth in your own spiritual life. Don't overthink it; just initiate contact and learn how to be a friend.

But what if they have children and their kids want my kids to be their friends? Even better, because now you get a chance to disciple your kids on the main command of Jesus. Kids of gay parents are going to grow up with incredible confusion, so why not make sure those kids always remember the Christian family next door who for some reason were the most loving people they'd ever met. Our job is not to convert people. Our job is to be a witness of Jesus to people. And if we have a true reconciler's heart—that is, we hope someday they will trust us enough to ask us about spiritual matters—then evangelism begins with changing their assumptions about what a Christian is.

But what if someone in my family is gay and the other members of the family are shunning him or her? Jesus was an advocate for sinners when they were under judgment or isolation from other religious people. Be it the woman caught in adultery or all the tax collectors in town, Jesus defended anyone who was ostracized or minimized, and He wants you to do the same. The best way to bring this up is not to bring it up but to simply engage those who are under judgment. The word will get out, and when other friends or family members bring it up (and they will), that's a really cool time to simply say, "I love him because I know God does." They may spit and sputter, and over time you'll either influence the way they think or you won't, but the person you are loving will always remember the Jesus follower who didn't judge him. And that will pay off.

But what if my gay friends ask me to attend their wedding? Go. This type of response would be great: "Wow, that's a huge day for you, and I'm honored you would ask." Then go and get to know as many folks as you can. In time, they will find out about your faith and think back to the day you came without judgment, and what will go through their heads will be, "$%!@, that's so cool that they are Christians and still came. I've never known anyone like them!" That's the beginning of a respectful relationship and ministry in their lives.

But what if they ask me what I think about their lifestyle? When you are friends, they will ask you. When that day comes, be honest and say, "I've noticed tons of stuff about your lifestyle, and I've found you to be warm, generous, caring, and thoughtful." (Remember, Genesis 1 is more important than Genesis 3. Their lifestyle isn't just about how they have sex. So always find ways to encourage the image of God you see in them.)

Then you can say, "I know you're really asking what I think about the way you have sex, so here's what I think. You know I follow Jesus, and I try to learn about God and life through the Bible. Obviously there are statements that cause Christians to believe that God created men and women physically compatible so that we can reproduce and fill the world. And I still believe that.

"But the Bible also mentions all sorts of other issues that prove I'm no better than you just because I am attracted to the opposite sex. I struggle with sexual issues heterosexually. I also struggle with greed, lying, selfishness, gluttony, and apathy. So I have absolutely no personal judgment about how you live your life. Jesus teaches people to be humble and honest and to come to Him for help, and that's what I'm doing. He also teaches that while I'm still working on issues in my own life, I should not judge others for things I can't understand. You are my friend, and I hope it stays that way, even if we don't believe the same things or live the same way. I really mean that."

But what if I'm a pastor and I just got asked to perform a gay wedding? First, congrats. That means you've been a good friend. Kudos for doing what Jesus asked you to! Okay, so this is a tough one. But before I throw in on this, let's remember that many pastors over the years have not even been willing to marry unbelievers. In fact, in Portland I was known as the pastor who actually would, and pastor after pastor sent people to me. Quite a few of these actually came to faith, and many became a part of our church. When someone asked one day why I marry people who aren't Christians, I replied, "Because God created marriage for humans, not just a certain strain of people. He also blessed marriage for about two thousand years before there were Christians. Another obvious reason is that marrying people is one of the most natural times to encourage them spiritually, so why would anyone who loves people limit their ability to do this?"

Most pastors belong to denominations that have a standing policy forbidding them from performing homosexual weddings, though. If this is your case, then you simply can't if your plan is to honor the commitment you made to your denomination. And that is your answer to a friend who asks. But if you are free from institutional constraints and still feel uncomfortable, then just be honest. In the times I've been asked, I've simply said something like, "Bill, you know I love you and am so honored you would ask me to do this for you. I know it is a huge day for you, and the fact that you asked me to play such a role in your life means the world to me. You know I don't judge you at all and that you are my friend forever. You also know, because I've been honest with you, that I'm still processing the issue of same-sex marriage. At this point of my processing, as much as I wish I were somewhere further down the road, I simply don't feel I have a clear conscience about sanctioning your union. I may change my mind someday, but it's where I'm at today, and I just want to be honest. Would you respect and accept where I am on this?" For me, this has worked out very well because it's completely honest and because I have built a good foundation of loving friendship.

Someone always asks, *Would you marry a believer and an unbeliever? I mean, the Bible is clear that people should not be yoked unequally, right?* Well, yes, God does give a good bit of wisdom about not overlooking issues of faith or religious differences in such an important decision as marriage. For sure our faith in Jesus is a whole-life orientation, so to marry someone who doesn't have similar convictions would seem to be in the "unwise" category. But remember, these scriptures are points of wisdom, not points by which to judge. My job as a friend or pastor is to give scriptural advice, but I don't feel I have the right to judge to the point of denying such a couple the right to something God has given them. This is their decision, not mine. I can give my input, and I can even warn or try to persuade someone from making this decision. But I cannot hold myself as judge and jury over who gets to be married. Heck, I've done hundreds of weddings, and many fully committed, equally yoked Christians are now divorced; many unbelievers are now believers; and many immature, semiequally, not so equally, and barely equally yoked people have grown in their faith, and my relationship and ministry to them was key to the process.

When we make judgments about who gets to do certain spiritual experiences, be it taking Communion, getting baptized, getting married, or getting buried with God's blessing, we are on dangerous ground. Remember the wheat and the chaff. This story encourages believers not to make judgments as to who's in and who's out. The main point is that God will straighten it all out in the end. In the meantime, it's our job not to separate, isolate, or legislate who gets to participate in spiritual experiences. If you want a much fuller discussion on why the Lord's Table, or Communion, should be more open, check out my book *Sacrilege*.

But what about marijuana? What if it becomes legal in my state? Trust me … it will. I live in Denver, so we're on the front edge of this, but it is coming. And this means that it may find its way into social gatherings you and your missionary friends will have. My guess is that you really won't have to worry too much because people will be far more discreet about its use than they are with alcohol. So if you handle booze well, weed won't be much of a problem.

But as with anything God created, it must be stewarded. People in your church and in your neighborhood will be smoking it, and if they ask you what you think, give them the same advice you would about any substance that can harm the body, mind, or a good party. Don't use it selfishly or irresponsibly. That's the best advice in all situations, and it pushes the issue of what Jesus would do and say back on them. If you let people take ownership of this decision, more times than not Jesus will speak to them, and you'll come off as a wise guide rather than a judgmental fuddy-duddy.

But here are some guides you can bring up when dealing with any substance.

We shouldn't do anything that we know will harm a weaker brother. So in that sense, I'd say you should never offer anything to someone you know is struggling with that substance. But you shouldn't avoid things because you *think* they may cause a problem. There are many things in life that screw people up. Men and women, money and the Internet, credit cards, even lawn mowers can all do some serious damage, but God doesn't outlaw them. He teaches us how to handle them all.

We should be moderate in our consumption of anything. Going overboard with doughnuts, alcohol, coffee, or chocolate-covered acai berries from Costco will always leave you regretful in the morning.

We are free to enjoy food and drink—even inhalants like cigs and cigars, hookahs and incense—if we can enjoy them responsibly and legally. Here's a crazy thought: God made the cannabis plant. "Yes, but He didn't mean for people to smoke it. It was supposed to be used for other stuff, like clothing and paper, right?" Well, if I'm God I'm going to assume that, eventually, people are going to burn just about anything they find. That means God knew a bunch of blokes clearing their fields would throw a couple of bushels of this stuff on an open flame and then wake up the next morning lying facedown next to their buddies. God knew almost every fruit He made would ferment and about a hundred plants would make you take a nap if ingested.

Don't do something your conscience struggles with or you don't actually enjoy. It always seems silly to me that people try to develop a taste for wine or beer (or kale, for that matter) just to fit in with a crowd. If you don't like the taste of something or if it makes you feel weird, uncomfortable, or keeps you from sleeping or makes you sleep at weird times, don't put it in your mouth or body. It's your life to live, so don't let people judge you, either.

But what about all this with my own kids? What happens when they get to the age when I can no longer look over their shoulder? And what if my children throw off all my wisdom and even chuck their faith? Do I just let them take the car keys, drive off, and screw up their life? I can't actually tell you how to parent, but I can give you a couple of thoughts to consider. All our kids are different. Some need pretty constant attention and clear boundaries while others need less. Regardless, the goal of good parenting is to help your children get to the place where they take ownership of their relationship with God and His way of life for themselves. While you are legally responsible for your kids (in most states that's up to eighteen years old), you're required by law to keep them in check. You have the right to withhold car keys, so if they want to mess up, they'll have to sneak out the window. But the sooner they learn a lesson the better, so at the point you feel they need to own their own life, it's probably better to give them the keys, let them screw up, and then be there when they come home. Not to tell them they suck or "I told you so" but to be like the prodigal father waiting for his delinquent son to return. This approach may not ensure a perfect upbringing or total security for your kids, but it will ensure your relationship with them remains in place, and that will win the day in the end.

But my neighbor, who is Muslim, asked me to come to his son's religious ceremony. Do we go, even though it's a religion that goes against our Christian faith? For sure. It is a huge honor to be able to be present with others in such intimate settings. You're going as a friend and a learner. Nothing bad can happen if that is your desire and motive.

Theological/Spiritual Issues

Hugh, I agree with you about judgment. But I really do care about the issue of hell and the people going there if they don't hear about God's truth and love. I have no desire to judge, but I really do love people and

have genuine concern for their eternal destiny. What do I do with this
tension?

Remember, it is the Holy Spirit's job to convince people of
their need for God. You cannot ever do this for Him. It's just too
hard. What you can do is make an already tough transition a bit
easier.

A few years ago I was driving down a highway by my home. Up
ahead I saw a ton of cars swerving and then pulling over into the
median. As I approached, I saw that one of the cars had struck and
wounded a deer. I thought people would help the injured animal,
but it looked like people were just frozen in fear. Some were crying,
a teenage girl was pacing frantically, and a few old folks were taking
pictures. I pulled over and quickly ran to the animal, which still
seemed dazed. I carefully picked him up under his belly and slowly
walked him step by step to the side of the road. I was hoping he
would get his feet under him and prance off into the woods, but he
just put his head on my lap to rest. Once the rubbernecking zombies
stopped freaking out, they began to come toward me and the deer. I
could feel the deer beginning to panic as they approached. I tried to
keep him calm by putting my hand out, signaling the people to stay
back, but they kept coming.

I quietly asked the first man there to stay back, keep the others
away, and call for an animal control agent. I was sure that if I could
just keep the deer with me, we could get him the help he needed.
But the man didn't listen, nor did the zombie crew fast approaching.
Eventually the deer just couldn't take it and bolted out of my arms,
struggling into the woods, where none of us were able to help. Two
days later, I saw him dead on the side of the road.

As with most things related to God, we can help a little, but we can hurt a lot. If you really want to help people to their eternal rest, help them with their earthly struggles and try to keep your spiritual conversations between friends. God is alpha and omega, and He is always bringing people into our lives. You are not the only voice, so focus on long-term, deeper relationships rather than drive-by conversations.

But what about judging other Christians? You might be thinking, "Hugh, actually most of my struggle isn't with outsiders, but the insiders. It kills me to have to constantly answer for the lousy experiences people have had with other Christians. Now I constantly fight the urge to just leave the tribe, punt, tap out, and go underground."

I get it, I really do. But included in the ones you can't write off are your Christian brothers and sisters. Yes, we've already talked about how we get a longer leash of confrontation within the church, but confronting a brother or sister still implies you've built a trusting relationship. Sure, I get upset when I see Facebook posts and news stories about Christians behaving badly, but I can't think of a single time it does any good to post a response to a stranger.

I hope these quick answers to the "buts" prove helpful. If other questions come up for you, feel free to go to hughhalter.com. You'll find a discussion board with other dilemmas, and I hope it is helpful for you as you represent Jesus.

What do we know for sure?
Or maybe not for sure?

• It is possible to live a life without judgment.

- However, because we live in a less-than-perfect world, the answers aren't always clear-cut. When questions arise, give yourself time to respond. If you don't have a good answer, simply say, "That's a great question, and I have no idea. How about you and I look at this together over the next month or so?"

What should we change in light of what we know?

- As Romans 12:18 says, "If it is possible, as far as it depends on you, live at peace with everyone." That's a good place to start. That means at least begin forming relationships with people you've historically stayed distant from. Better to learn how to deal with messy situations than have no mess at all.

- In every situation, we can choose how we react. The world is what it is. To become a nonjudger, you have to learn to laugh at the human race instead of wishing it would change. Someday it will be fixed! Jesus promises.

Who might this change affect, and what is God asking you to do?

- Reconciliation doesn't always work; at times it will fail because reconciliation takes two people agreeing to come together. Often you will be the only one bent on doing so. Give yourself a break. At least you are trying or have tried.

Why is this good news for you?

- If you live your life as a friend and a learner, rather than a judger, you will represent Jesus well ... and possibly change lives.

THE FINAL APPEAL

*We may not all be on the same chapter, but
we should be in the same book.*

—R. Alan Woods

As we finish up, I want to give you some personal thoughts. When we started, I declared that I am a recovering Pharisee. I've judged people my whole life, and I didn't want you to feel like I was putting a finger in your chest as much as I was using my own struggles to help you think about judgment for yourself.

My heart behind this effort is for the good news of Jesus, through His church, to have a deep, long-lasting effect on people. I want Jesus to be made famous. I want my daughters and their daughters to find a movement of people that they deeply respect and want to be a part of. And I ultimately hope that as the people of God are transformed, the fate of the church will follow suit.

I know I could not address all the issues you face as you live and work in the real world, but I hope we've covered enough to settle some of the questions, to soften your posture with the world, and to give you some good news for your own life in Jesus. Here are a few final thoughts I feel God spoke to me while I wrote this book.

Err on the Side of Love

First of all, for most of my life I thought the job of a Christian was to err on the side of truth. As with most of my evangelical friends, I've overlooked the many hundreds of scriptures that speak about love and instead used one or two scriptures like "The church … [is] the pillar and foundation of the truth" (1 Tim. 3:15) to defend and justify my lack of love and acceptance of people. If I made truth the main thing, then I didn't have to worry about my posture with people—I didn't have to relate to them, befriend them, or include them in my life. But as a father and a friend, I've learned that truth is received only when it is presented from a posture of love. I don't believe love is more important than truth, but I now believe that love must come before truth. That's what the incarnation of Jesus shows us. He came as love to us, as a friend, and therefore (meaning, after that) we began to accept His truth.

I am worried, of course, that my writing *Brimstone* will cause people I care about to question my commitment to conservative Christian values and morals. But I'm even more concerned about meeting my true judge someday—seeing Jesus face-to-face. And now that I've seen, and tried to show you, that Jesus puts the law of love over all other laws, I feel comfortable to err on the side of friendship and love with the world. If I make the wrong call on the truth, if I become too "liberal" in some people's minds, and if I miss opportunities to confront and challenge people with sin, I feel that at least I can stand before Jesus and say, "I only tried to do what You said was the main thing. I tried at all costs to be and stay their friend. I tried to always show grace and patience. In Your name, I never wanted to belittle them or cause them to feel I was any better than them. For sure, I always wanted to keep the relationship open so that as Your Spirit did the work of convicting and convincing, I would never make Your job harder."

I hope that you, too, will choose the side of love. Since judgment requires you to pick a side, I hope you choose love, not *over* truth, but *before* truth.

First Corinthians 13 really isn't a sappy wedding scripture. It's like a monastic creed or code of chivalry that becomes an oath of commitment when someone loves the King and His kingdom. Codes, oaths, and creeds are not just words on paper. They are plumb lines for behavior. Nonjudgment is not an idea. It is an action. Thus:

Love is patient. It lets people struggle through their journey. It doesn't demand immediate change.

Love is kind. When they live in the exact opposite way that you would, you still smile, speak softly and gently, and be a friend.

Love doesn't envy or boast; it's not proud or rude. Love isn't shown through superiority or competition, nor does it make people feel bad or belittled.

Love isn't self-seeking, so it has no personal agenda for people.

It's not easily angered, so you're going to have to let quite a few drops of irritation roll off your back and actually resign yourself not to bring them up to try to get closure.

And this one will be really tough, but *love doesn't keep a list of anything*, especially bad things, failures, sins, or screwups. So love never says, "I told you so," or "you got what you deserve."

Love doesn't rejoice in evil. So you can't actually be happy when someone's sin finds him or her out. You should be sad when sin wins the day and evil gets a laugh.

Love always covers sins and protects someone's public image. So love doesn't Facebook the frailties of people. Rather, it always trusts God to continue His work in people's lives. It always hopes for God to get through to them and just hangs in there. Love never misses a day of prayer and always keeps the vertical relationship strong so that God can include you in helping someone find the light.

Creating Children of Light

Second, I want to encourage you to look for fruit rather than justification for your judgments. In that key verse in Luke 7:34, we read, "The Son of Man came eating and drinking, and you say, 'Here is a glutton and a drunkard, a friend of tax collectors and sinners.'" This scripture passage ends with a very interesting statement, though: "But wisdom is proved right by all her children" (v. 35).

What Jesus was saying is essentially this: "I know you have based your life on the laws of God, the laws of Moses, and the Scriptures as you've been taught and come to own. I know you're just trying to be faithful to what you think is right, but you will ultimately know truth and wisdom by what works. The offspring of your behavior and judgments show that you are making disciples who don't live like Jesus. You can stand apart from the sinners and continue to picket their lifestyles, or you can become a real friend. I think after ten years of trying both options, you'll see more fruit, more children of light, by heading down the friendship route!"

Wisdom is proving that our Bible-thumping judgments are not winning the day. You'd have to check your brain at the door if you think we should keep being Christians and doing church the way we have been. There's simply no wisdom in staying the same when we're daily losing respect and our own members by the thousands. Wisdom shows that the Christian movement in the West is dangerously close to losing its saltiness, and the Scriptures warn that once we've lost our ability to preserve and influence, we won't get it back. While we may continue to keep our church attendance, our Bibles, our worship services, and small groups going as usual, if we don't become more like Jesus, nothing we do in His name will be effective.

Jesus proved that if you live a holy life without judgment, you will win hearts and see lives changed. Anything less or different won't do. So if you look at your own life and see little fruit of lost friends finding life in Jesus, consider the friendship route. You have nothing to lose, there is enough scripture on your side, and on the day you face Jesus, you'll have an honest heart as you explain why you lived the way you did.

Take Scripture more seriously. I guess you could boil this entire book down to one story Jesus told. In Matthew 13:24–30 Jesus summarizes why we never have to worry about judging.

> Jesus told them another parable: "The kingdom of
> heaven is like a man who sowed good seed in his
> field. But while everyone was sleeping, his enemy

came and sowed weeds among the wheat, and went away. When the wheat sprouted and formed heads, then the weeds also appeared.

"The owner's servants came to him and said, 'Sir, didn't you sow good seed in your field? Where then did the weeds come from?'

"'An enemy did this,' he replied.

"The servants asked him, 'Do you want us to go and pull them up?'

"'No,' he answered, 'because while you are pulling the weeds, you may uproot the wheat with them. Let both grow together until the harvest. At that time I will tell the harvesters: First collect the weeds and tie them in bundles to be burned; then gather the wheat and bring it into my barn.'"

The parable is pretty self-explanatory, so at this point I don't really need to comment, but it is helpful to know that the main question we will always have is this: Shall we pull out the weeds? And Jesus's response will always be what the farmer said: No, you'll hurt the wheat if you do. We'll sort it out during the harvest.

Jesus did the same thing in Luke 9:54, when His own disciples got angry that people weren't responding to Him and self-righteously asked, "Lord, do you want us to call fire down from heaven to destroy them?" But Jesus turned and rebuked them.

In both cases, Jesus intentionally gives us permission not to worry about the situation or the person but instead to let Him work it out.

Bema Seat: Your Final Judgment

The Scriptures do speak of a final day of judgment called the *bema seat*. Fortunately, you will not be judged for your sin because Jesus already took care of it. The judgment instead will be about how you lived since Jesus got you off the hook. In other words, you're not going to be judged based on whether you are free or not, but on what you did with the freedom Jesus gave you.

Unlike an ex-con who gets out of jail after paying his penalty and then uses his freedom to serve only himself, we are invited to live in the freedom of Christ to help others also find freedom in him. If being a disciple means that Christ is being formed in us, and if, as Paul says, we have been crucified with Christ so it's no longer us who live but Jesus living in us, and if it's true that the hope of glory—that is, the hope of God for the world—is Christ in us, then we have an unprecedented opportunity to walk in the world exactly like Jesus did.

So in answer to the question at the very beginning as to whether Jesus would bake a wedding cake for the gay couple, I'd say *yes*, He would. He has baked the cake for all of us. While we were yet sinners, sinning daily, screwed up to the deepest level, stiff-arming Him and His grace, Christ died for us. He went to our parties, drove us home when we were drunk, washed the vomit off our clothes, and tucked us in bed. And then the next morning He made us breakfast and gently helped us to the table where He could share a few helpful words. Yes, He goes to our weddings too. He hangs back as a gentleman and lets us live our lives for ourselves, pursuing all the empty trash the world has to offer. He holds His tongue until we ask for help and never interrupts our boisterous ramblings. He's just always there, like a perfect friend.

Considering all this, for us who have had our cake and eaten it too, let us live as a true aroma of Christ instead of a stench or fume of brimstone.

If it is Christ in us, if God is making His appeal through us, then why do we keep trying to protect our image and our values? We should instead be image bearers and let people be with us so they can pick up on our values.

May wisdom be proved right! May the church come alive! And may you live like Jesus.

Hugh

NOTES

3 Don't Be a Stoner: Time to Drop the Rocks

1. Debra Hirsch, *Redeeming Sex: Naked Conversations about Sexuality and Spirituality* (Downers Grove, IL: IVP Books, 2015).

2. Alan and Debra Hirsch, *Untamed: Reactivating a Missional Form of Discipleship* (Grand Rapids, MI: Baker, 2010), 225.

4 Hinge Point: The World Hangs in the Balance

1. Glenn McEntyre, "Topless Exotic Dancers Begin Weekly Protests at Central Ohio Church," WBNS-10TV, August 10, 2014, www.10tv.com/content/stories/2014/08/10/warsaw-ohio --topless-exotic-dancers-begin-weekly-protests-at-central-ohio -church.html.

2. Dietrich Bonhoeffer, *The Cost of Discipleship* (New York: Touchstone, 1995), 96–98.

5 Missing-ology: Nonjudgment 401

1. N.T. Wright, "How Can the Bible Be Authoritative?" (Laing Lecture 1989, and the Griffith Thomas Lecture 1989). Originally published in *Vox Evangelica* (1991), 21: 7–32.

7 Our Clandestine Calling: Rethinking Reconciliation

1. Jon Foreman, quoted in Tim Challies, "Another Switchfoot Concert," July 10, 2004, www.challies.com/music-movies/another-switchfoot-concert.

2. Penn Jillette, "A Gift of a Bible," YouTube video, 5:11, posted by "beinzee," July 8, 2010, www.youtube.com/watch?v=6md638smQd8.